Practical Reiki

Practical Reiki

*Focus Your Body's Energy
for Deep Relaxation
and Inner Peace*

Richard Ellis

Sterling Publishing Co., Inc.
New York
A Sterling/Silver Book

A QUARTO BOOK

QUAR.RKI

Conceived, designed, and produced by:
Quarto Publishing plc
The Old Brewery
6 Blundell Street
London N7 9BH

Editor **Sarah Vickery**
Art editor **Sally Bond**
Assistant art director **Penny Cobb**
Designer **Ruth Hope**
Photographer **Colin Bowling**
Illustrator **Chen Ling**
Picture researcher **Laurent Boubounelle**
Indexer **Dawn Butcher**

Art director **Moira Clinch**
Publisher **Piers Spence**

Contents

"How do you make God laugh? Tell him your plans."

Introduction

IN 1992 I WAS LIVING IN LONDON, working as a photographer in the fashion and music industries. This had been my goal since leaving college in 1983, and after a lot of hard work things were at last coming together. But despite my growing professional success, I had a nagging sense that something was missing from my life.

From my earliest childhood I had always been curious as to why I was here. I had been lucky enough to grow up in Africa, where the very closeness of nature instills a deep respect for all things living.

I was always happiest in the great outdoors. London, by contrast, I found a difficult place to live in: deprived of horizons and sunsets, I felt truly cut off from nature. Looking back now at this sense of alienation I recognize that deep transformational forces were at work within me. Change was coming and I was powerless to stop it.

In early 1993 I had the first of a number of transcendental experiences. I was walking along a quiet road in a small town in the French Alps, having spent the evening with friends.

As I looked up at the winter night sky and saw a hundred billion stars twinkling, something shifted in me. It was as if I had caught a glimpse of my intimate connection with everything else in the universe. I felt enveloped in the warm glow of an overpowering love. This profoundly moving experience stayed with me for days.

On my return to London I knew that something inside me had changed forever. By chance I met a succession of people who had experienced this same sense of oneness. Soon I was swept up in a wave of New Age consciousness: this was a very confusing time for me and yet I felt sure it was right.

Reawakening

Later that year I visited the Findhorn Community in Scotland, where I experienced a sense of communion so intense that it was at times almost too much to bear. I realized that I had spent years developing a hardness around my heart to enable me to function in the world. Suddenly it was breaking down: the flood gates were opening, and I could do nothing but surrender. Five days into my stay I was taken to a hill known as the Power Point, a place where many ley lines intersect. What occurred there threw my whole perception of reality into doubt: I experienced such powerful surges of physical energy that I felt as if I had been plugged into a power supply. My whole body vibrated with electricity; I found it almost impossible to breathe, and great sobs emanated from deep within me. Of our group, only I felt this energy, and I found this confusing. For a week or two I walked around with a Messiah complex; then I began to worry about my state of mind. Finally, I tried to forget the whole thing.

But I couldn't put it out of my head. The next thing I knew, everyone I met seemed to be involved in healing in one way or another. I'm hitchhiking and the person who picks me up turns out to be a healer. Or I get into conversation with someone in a bar and they've just been to see a healer. Someone was trying hard to get my attention.

One day I noticed a woman sitting next to me on the bus holding her stomach and heart with her hands. Intrigued, I asked what she was doing. "Reiki," came the reply. She told me as much as she could and I was fascinated. A week later a friend called. There was one place left on a Reiki course in Findhorn: would I like to have it? I thought about it and agreed to let her know within a day or two. The following morning I received two letters in the post. The first contained background information about Reiki, and to this day I don't know who sent it. The second was from the woman I had met on the bus. How much more convincing did I need?

Introduction to Reiki

When I met June Woods, my Reiki master, I was struck by her gentleness and by the warmth of her touch. As she introduced me to Reiki, I knew that I had found what had been missing. There were no fireworks and flashing lights – simply a profound sense of coming home. Everything she taught me seemed deeply familiar and felt right. I remember lying in bed with my hands on my heart, energy pouring into me. I knew that I had received more than a healing system. I had a connection to spirit that would become the mainstay of my life.

I returned to London and practiced on everyone I knew. I felt a real sense of purpose growing within me and tried to channel this energy into my work as a photographer. My images changed, I noticed: they became cleaner and simpler than before. But try as I might, I found it hard to integrate my new-found spiritual life with my professional one. I struggled on in London, but it seemed that every unit of effort was reaping fewer rewards than before. Eventually I found myself so broke that it seemed a decision was being forced on me.

At the back of my mind I knew I wanted to take the master level. I discussed it with my master and resolved to spend a week in retreat meditating on the decision. During one of these meditations I had a vision of a tall man who looked a bit like Merlin wearing a hat and a long coat. He smiled as he approached. I asked him what I should do, at which he laughed and said: "You know very well what you should do. The question is: do you have the courage?" With that he was gone.

Later that month I received the master initiation from June Woods. It is hard to describe the sensation of energy that filled me, seeming to expand my being beyond anything I could have imagined. It was as if June had stepped inside me and a whole queue of people behind her did the same. I remember floating about for a few days in a complete state of bliss. Within three weeks of my initiation I had closed my business in London, sold most of my belongings, rented out my flat, and gone to live in a two-man tent in rainy Scotland. I am sure most of my friends and family had decided that I had lost touch with reality. But the exact opposite was true: I was never more in touch. I found my solace in a pack of Angel cards. Time after time I picked the same cards: Trust, Faith, and Courage.

The power of Reiki

Four years later I look back at that time with great fondness. The death and transformation of one's former beliefs and identity is never easy. The Tibetans talk of impermanence, of approaching each moment as if it is your last. The profound connection I had discovered to spirit through Reiki motivated me to surrender to the flow of my life. When I needed support the energy enveloped me with love.

Today I try to travel light; I become uneasy when my belongings get to be more than I can carry. I teach all around the world, but mainly in London and Italy. I never cease to be amazed at the power of Reiki as a transformational healing tool. I continue to grow and learn from those I teach, and Reiki is the power that supports that growth.

I hope that you will find this book a useful reference point at whatever stage you might have reached in your discovery of the world of energy. In drawing from my personal experience of working with Reiki, I present my ideas as guidelines that have worked for me. I hope they encourage you to find your own way toward truth and help you in your healing.

Chapter 1

What is Reiki?

Chapter 1

*"It is better to light
a single candle
than curse the darkness"*

CHINESE PROVERB

Reiki is

• *a system of energy healing using spiritually guided life force energy*

• *a useful tool for self-awareness and transformation*

• *a non-invasive therapy*

• *practiced throughout the world*

> *"One fish says to another: 'Do you believe in this ocean they talk about?"*

CHINESE PROVERB

• *a continuation of teachings given by Reiki Grand Master Dr Usui at the end of the nineteenth century*

• *an honoring of the Dr Usui lineage*

• *used in hospitals, private practice, self care, and in conjunction with many other therapies*

Reiki is not

• *affiliated with any one religion or religious practice*

Defining qualities of Reiki

- *practiced by transmitting healing energy through the hands*
- *passed on through the initiation process from master to student*
- *healing energy that is guided spiritually*
- *not based on belief, faith, or suggestion*

REIKI IS A SYSTEM OF HEALING that originated in Japan and dates back to the end of the nineteenth century. It is practiced by the simple process of laying on of hands to channel healing energy through the practitioner to the recipient. This healing can take place on many levels.

Rei: the whole of creation

Reiki is a Japanese word that translates as "God Light Energy". The easiest way to understand its true meaning is to split the word in two. Rei is directly translated as God or light. It is used to describe the whole of creation—every cell, blade of grass, stone, tree, animal, human, every planet and star. It goes further to describe the creative mind of God. An accurate interpretation of the word Rei could be "All That Is," both in thought and form.

Ki: life energy

Ki is the name given to the vital energy that is used to animate and give life to this creation. Just as a model car requires batteries to make it move, so the complex creation of the universe requires a form of energy to animate it. This energy, also known as chi or prana, can be viewed as an ocean that surrounds the physical universe. It provides us with the vitality we require to maintain our health, balance, and well being on all levels—physical, emotional, mental, and spiritual.

Ki can normally be seen with the naked eye, and appears as dancing electrons of light that move rapidly around. There is an abundance of this energy in nature, and it is most clearly visible in mountainous areas, at the ocean's edge, or in dense forests. Most forms of martial arts, in particular Ki Gong and Tai Chi, acknowledge the presence of this energy and focus on redistributing ki throughout the body to increase health, balance, and well-being.

What can Reiki teach us?

Reiki is a system of healing that has been developed to bring us directly into contact with the creative intelligence and the vital energy of the universe. This is achieved through a series of transmissions from a Reiki teacher, designed to re-connect us to this universal ki. It is then practiced by developing our awareness of our own energetic self and bringing ki into ourselves to revitalize our body and free it from emotional issues, belief systems, and physical disorders that no longer serve us. As our ability increases and our awareness grows we can allow this energy to flow through us for the benefit of others.

Reiki teaches us that pain, suffering, and illness is caused by separation from the oneness of creation on some level. In other words, it is our loneliness, our feelings of isolation, that cause the pain and suffering. We are on a planet spinning around a solar system and we don't really know where we are going. To most people this is such a frightening realization that it is far easier to completely block it out and focus their attention on something less immediate.

Re-connecting with ourselves

Deep down, however, it has its effect. If we are honest, most of us have asked ourselves: "What did I do to deserve this? What am I doing here? How did I end up on this planet, surrounded by complete strangers?" The fact is that everyone is feeling the same, and this knowledge is the first step in realizing that we all have something in common. We are all lonely, and the more we strain our eyes looking through telescopes in the hope of finding someone else, the more this only serves to increase this feeling of isolation. We are looking outwardly for something that isn't there. We are looking in the wrong direction.

Reiki is a way of bringing us back home, of re-connecting with the essence of who we are. Reiki is a way to remove the veil that prevents us from experiencing the union with the divine. As we begin to wake up to this idea and walk its path the veil becomes thinner and thinner. We begin to see that it was our fears and beliefs in limitation that created the veil in the first place. So Reiki is a doorway that can re-connect us to the very place we came from. Reiki is a doorway home.

Reiki in Japanese
Above The Japanese script shows the symbols for the word "Reiki".

The chakra system

I HAVE TALKED ABOUT THE OCEAN OF ENERGY that we operate within, and how it can support us energetically. However, for this to happen a mechanism known as the chakra system is required. The chakras are centers throughout the body that act like lungs, breathing vital energy from the ocean of energy into our system and distributing it throughout the body along channels known as nadis. Chakra is Sanskrit for wheel, and this serves to describe the spinning motion that the chakras employ to draw this energy into our being.

THE PHYSICAL RELATIONSHIP

There are seven main chakra centers throughout the body, each one having a direct relationship to the part of the physical body it governs. The corresponding system on the physical body is called the endocrine system.

The chakra system is made up of a single vertical power channel, running from the top of the head (the crown center) down the spine, to the coccyx (the base center). These two chakras at each end of the spine open out like funnels from the narrow vertical channel. This vertical power current forms our connection to spirit and earth. Along this vertical current are five chakras, forming horizontal intersections evenly distributed along its length. Each of these appears as a pair, with one facing the front and the other facing the back. Viewed from the side these look like open-ended funnels, radiating out from the spinal column.

Funnels of power
Below The seven chakra centers in the body take the form of funnels that radiate out from the spinal column.

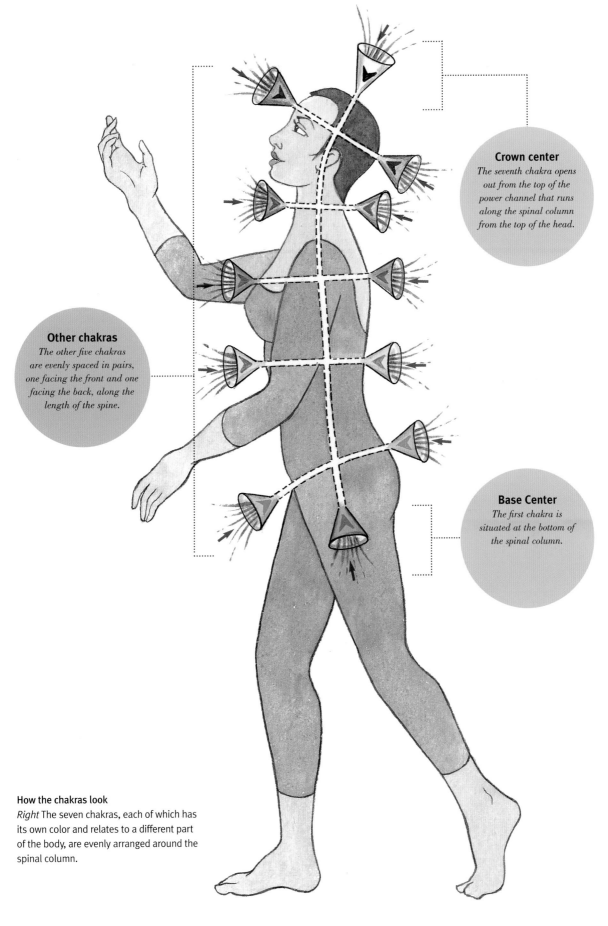

Crown center
The seventh chakra opens out from the top of the power channel that runs along the spinal column from the top of the head.

Other chakras
The other five chakras are evenly spaced in pairs, one facing the front and one facing the back, along the length of the spine.

Base Center
The first chakra is situated at the bottom of the spinal column.

How the chakras look
Right The seven chakras, each of which has its own color and relates to a different part of the body, are evenly arranged around the spinal column.

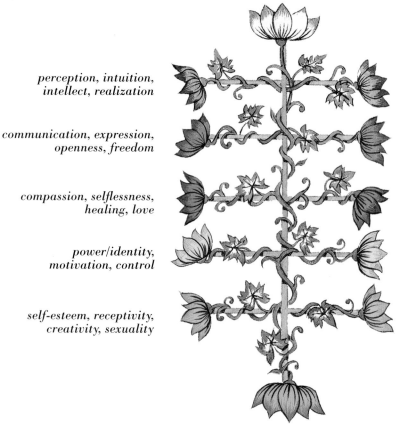

spirit
union, impermanence,
contemplation, wholeness

perception, intuition,
intellect, realization

communication, expression,
openness, freedom

compassion, selflessness,
healing, love

power/identity,
motivation, control

self-esteem, receptivity,
creativity, sexuality

earth
trust/security,
grounding, stability

Tree of life
Left As well as connecting with the physical body, each chakra has a corresponding psychological and emotional issue. We pass through these on our journey through life.

THE EMOTIONAL AND PSYCHOLOGICAL RELATIONSHIP

In addition to the chakras' relationship with the physical body, each also has a relationship to our emotional and psychological selves. We develop each chakra for a period of seven years, before moving on to the next one. This begins at birth, as we emerge from the protection of our mother's womb and start to develop our relationship with the outside world. The chakras represent a journey beginning at the base, or 1st chakra, and moving up through each chakra in turn every seven years, until at the age of 43 we arrive at the crown. At the end of our 49th year the cycle is complete and we return again to the first chakra.

In this way, the chakras can be seen as a logical progression through life as we learn to deal with the outside world and its relationship with our own inner world. The soul incarnates in the physical world, which is represented by the vertical line from spirit to Earth. Then the soul goes through five levels of interaction with the world as it develops its physical, emotional, psychological, and spiritual self.

Emotional connections
Right Our emotional development throughout life corresponds to our cycle through the seven chakras, each one lasting seven years from birth to the age of 49. The heart is the central chakra, through which the universal love radiates.

THE SEVEN MAIN CHAKRAS AND THEIR RELATED ASPECTS

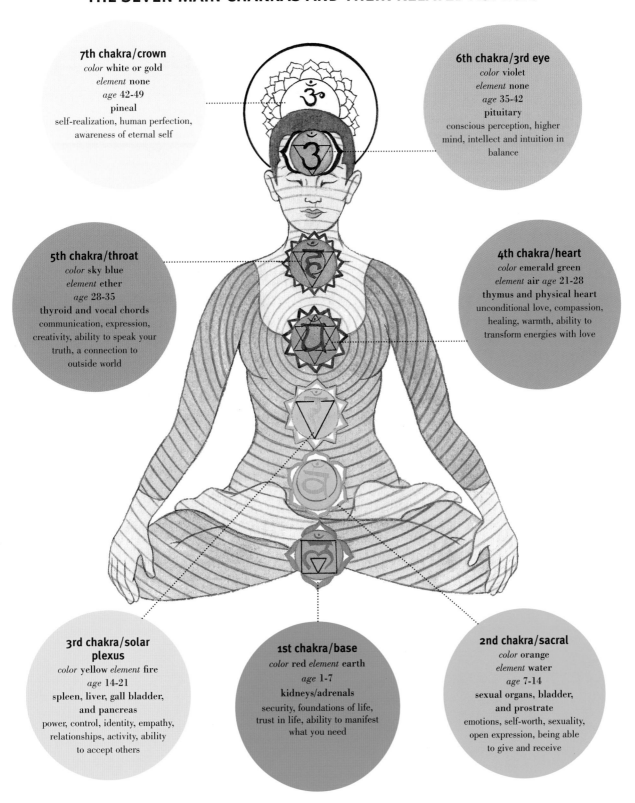

7th chakra/crown
color white or gold
element none
age 42-49
pineal
self-realization, human perfection,
awareness of eternal self

6th chakra/3rd eye
color violet
element none
age 35-42
pituitary
conscious perception, higher
mind, intellect and intuition in
balance

5th chakra/throat
color sky blue
element ether
age 28-35
thyroid and vocal chords
communication, expression,
creativity, ability to speak your
truth, a connection to
outside world

4th chakra/heart
color emerald green
element air *age* 21-28
thymus and physical heart
unconditional love, compassion,
healing, warmth, ability to
transform energies with love

**3rd chakra/solar
plexus**
color yellow *element* fire
age 14-21
spleen, liver, gall bladder,
and pancreas
power, control, identity, empathy,
relationships, activity, ability
to accept others

1st chakra/base
color red *element* earth
age 1-7
kidneys/adrenals
security, foundations of life,
trust in life, ability to manifest
what you need

2nd chakra/sacral
color orange
element water
age 7-14
sexual organs, bladder,
and prostrate
emotions, self-worth, sexuality,
open expression, being able
to give and receive

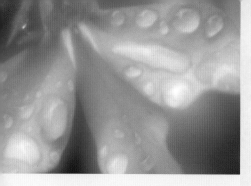

The **energetic body**

AS WELL AS THE PHYSICAL LAYER around the human body, there are believed to be seven further layers, which increase in vibration the further from the physical they are. These layers are refered to as the energetic bodies. For the purpose of our work I will simplify these down to three layers.

- *the etheric body*
  - *the emotional body*
    - *the mental body*

THE ETHERIC BODY

The first of these bodies is known as the etheric body. This is visible to most people as an aura around the physical body of a person, extending out to approximately 2 in. It appears to the naked eye as moving light, almost flame-like, and constantly in motion.

The etheric body draws vital energy from the ocean of energy through the solar plexus chakra and distributes this energy, via the chakra system and nadis, into the physical body. When the body is receiving healthy amounts of vital energy this will be reflected in the strength of the etheric field around it. This etheric body can be photographed using a technique known as Kirlian photography. The etheric field is made up of rays of light that radiate out from the physical. The stronger the rays emitted the more vitality is contained in the physical. These rays of light make up a protective web of light around the physical and appear to be magnetically charged and polarized. In a healthy state they appear straight but when disrupted can become tangled or bent.

Nurturing your etheric body

Our interaction with nature is an important part of nurturing our etheric bodies, as trees, flowers and plants have similar etheric bodies to our own and can be used to recharge our energy. You may find sitting with your back to a tree or smelling and breathing in the scents of flowers to be of great benefit. Conversely, spending time around electrical appliances like computers, mobile telephones, and televisions can have a negative effect on you as they scramble the electromagnetic field of energy around you. This is due to the high levels of electromagnetic radiation emitted by such devices. If you must be around these devices then regular breaks are important. In addition, unhealthy lifestyles with the abuse of drugs or alcohol can also have a detrimental effect on the strength of this body. One of the most powerful healing aspects of Reiki is in maintaining high levels of vitality within this etheric body. This will serve to protect you from illness and disruptive electromagnetic radiation whenever it enters your field of energy. It will also be of great benefit in helping you clear such external invasions from your field. We will talk about how this is possible in the chapter on First Degree Reiki.

Energy on film

Kirlian photography is a unique system that enables us to record the etheric energy field of the body on film. The photographs are, in effect, negative images where light is represented by black and vice versa. It is of great benefit to be able to show the effects of Reiki on the energy field, as these examples show.

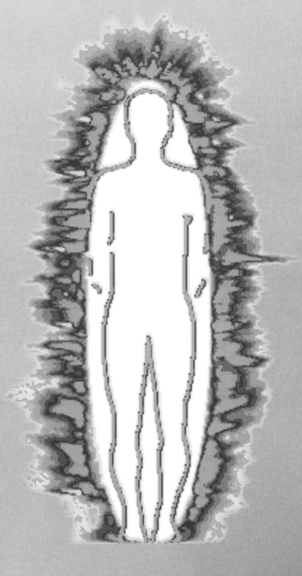

The perfect etheric body
Right and below These images show the etheric, emotional, and mental energy fields of a balanced and healthy person. The etheric field is closest to the physical body.

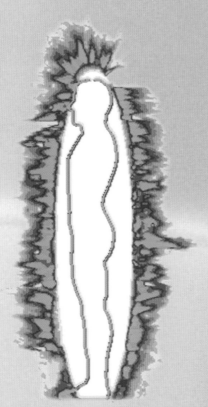

> *"The world is a movie: we are the director, the producer, we play the lead role, we choose the cast, the location, and manage the budget. We write the script as we go along and it can be changed whenever we wish"*

Relationships

The dynamic of "like attracts like" is played out most often in our personal relationships. When we feel a very strong attraction to a person we are literally pulled together by an energy interaction taking place in our emotional fields. We experience this as falling in love. We move on to the bliss of union, for what is commonly called the honeymoon period. Then things start to change: issues start to surface as our partner reflects back to us our deepest, unconscious fears about relationships. Trust, ownership, betrayal, freedom, anger, and fear can begin to surface.

THE EMOTIONAL BODY

The second layer of the energetic body is known as the emotional body, which reflects the emotional state of the person. Those people who have developed their ability to see energy fields report this body as being made up of colors that are constantly changing, and radiate out from the physical body from 1 $1/_2$–5 ft (0.5–1m), depending on the person being viewed. These colors change depending on the emotions being experienced. Emotions such as anger and fear will appear as dark clouds, whereas love and joy will appear as bright, glowing colors.

The emotional signature

In addition to immediate feelings and emotions, the emotional body holds all the unresolved emotional conflicts and fears relating back to a person's early life. These fears and conflicts are transmitted to the external world, via the chakras, as an unconscious message. We refer to this as the emotional signature of a person, and the simple rule of "like attracts like" reflects this message. The signature we send out into the world will act like a magnet, drawing us to situations and experiences that reflect our unconscious fears and emotions. In this way, the world can be seen as a mirror in which to observe our own unconscious self.

If somebody is unconsciously angry then the people or situations they attract will reflect that anger. They might consider themself to be loving and peaceful, while unconsciously sending out deeply aggressive energy signals. The signals they are sending out will draw experiences to them that reflect this aggression.

The purpose of this mirroring is to bring our unresolved issues up onto the conscious level. Once we are aware of the signals we are sending out into the world, and understand the law of attraction, we can begin to take responsibility and start to change them.

Reiki plays an important part in this process. When we receive Reiki it gives us high vibrational energy, which works to stimulate low vibrational clouds in our emotional body and make them vibrate at higher and higher rates. As they vibrate higher the memory of the experiences that caused the clouds to be formed is released, allowing us to re-experience it and forgive ourselves and the people involved. The memory held in the emotional body, and its effect on the physical body, is then released, and we can unfurl like a closed leaf, reaching full growth as emotionally healthy beings.

Radiating energy
Below The energy field of the emotional body is made up of colors that constantly change according to the emotions being experienced. Feelings of joy, fear, and conflict are transmitted by the seven chakras.

1 1st chakra/base
2 2nd chakra/sacral
3 3rd chakra/solar plexus
4 4th chakra/heart
5 5th chakra/throat
6 6th chakra/3rd eye
7 7th chakra/crown

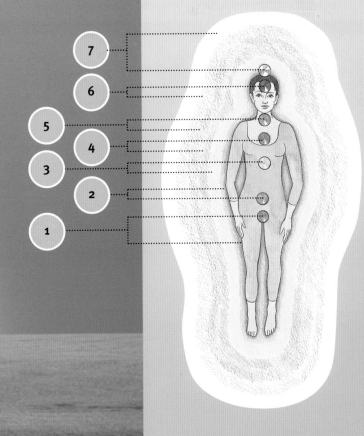

THE MENTAL BODY

The third layer of the energetic body is known as the mental body, which radiates out to around 9 ft (3m) around the physical body. This field of energy holds our beliefs about reality, formed throughout our lives. Belief systems reflect the culture we have been brought up in, the beliefs we have inherited from our parents, our religion, and our peer groups. The mental body reflects our rational mind and perceptions on a physical level. The experiences we have in the physical body are processed in the mental body after having passed through the emotional body. Therefore, our perceptions and rational thoughts are often deeply affected by any unresolved issues on the emotional level.

This field of energy is very much like a transmitter and receiver. We pick up on the thought projections of the people around us, and the unconscious messages being sent into the world through sources such as television and newspapers. These projections are often fearful and concerned with worldly matters. We absorb these and hold them in our own energy field—we start to believe they belong to us. Our own perception of the world can then become clouded by this invasion of negative thought patterns, and we will find our attention becomes focused on these issues.

What we think is what we become. When we send our beliefs about ourselves out into the world, they are reflected back to confirm our thoughts. So if we believe the world is a dark place, and that we are powerless victims of it, the world will oblige us by reflecting our beliefs and presenting us with situations and people that support these beliefs.

The true function of the mental body is to marry the conscious mind with intuitive perception. Once we are aware of our access to the mind of God we are able to respond to the information and signals we receive on an intuitive level and translate them into a more solid form. So, as our chakra system suggests, we are a bridge between spirit and earth, and part of our function is to access the information given by spirit and utilize it here on earth. The cleansing of the emotional body of its unresolved issues is vital for this process to take place without distortion. While we may receive clear and precise guidance, our own issues can distort this information or manipulate it to serve our own needs. Our beliefs can also block this perception, as it may threaten our limited view of reality.

Ripples in a pond

In meditation, I was shown how thoughts are like ripples in a still pond. Once formed they are sent out in all directions. I was invited to play with different thoughts—positive and negative—to show me their different qualities. I was shocked and amazed at how real they were. It was as if I could touch them.

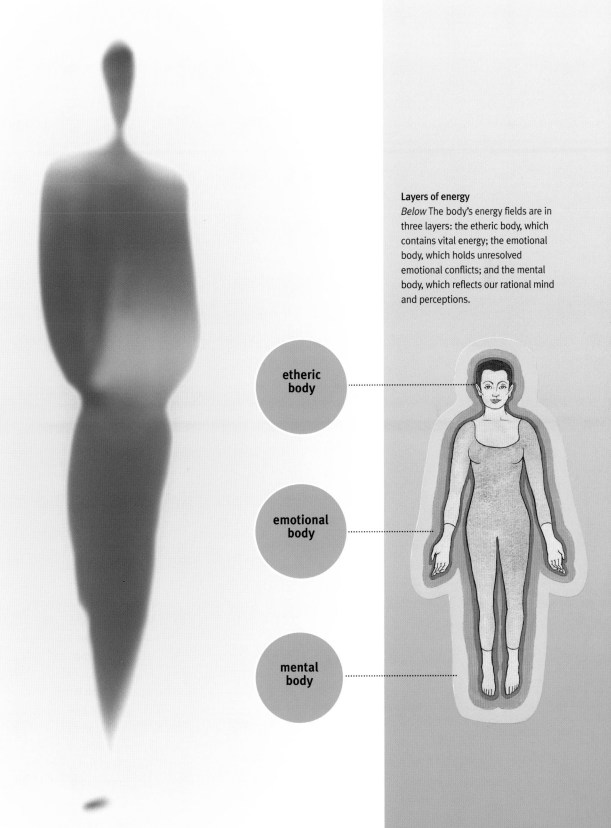

Layers of energy

Below The body's energy fields are in three layers: the etheric body, which contains vital energy; the emotional body, which holds unresolved emotional conflicts; and the mental body, which reflects our rational mind and perceptions.

etheric body

emotional body

mental body

How is dysfunction caused?

As the description of the chakras and the energetic bodies demonstrates, our lives are a journey, and during this journey we develop ourselves on all levels. The outside world and the people around us play an important role in the shaping of who we are, both emotionally and in terms of our beliefs about the world. As we grow up we develop emotional patterns that are based on the patterns of those people. We also inherit the belief systems of our immediate environment, so in a sense we begin to mimic the behaviour of others as a way of validating our own beliefs. We learn how to function in the world through the teachings and guidance we receive from those around us.

CASE STUDY

From birth to the age of seven, our subject is developing her base chakra, and if her basic needs are not met by her parents, she will begin to lose trust in her ability to survive. At the age of eight she moves into the next stage of her development, her second chakra, and is working on issues such as sexuality, self-worth, feelings, and emotions. She is looking to expand her horizons, she wants to fit in with her peer group, and her self-worth depends on it.

At the age of nine our child's parents move home. Suddenly she is ripped away from the surroundings that are familiar to her. She has already developed issues relating to security and trust, and now they are enforced with a new set of issues.

At the age of fifteen our subject moves into her third chakra. She is working with issues of control, power, and her personal identity. She is, however, very fragile, as she carries unconscious fears that the world is a dangerous place, and is still very dependent on her parents.

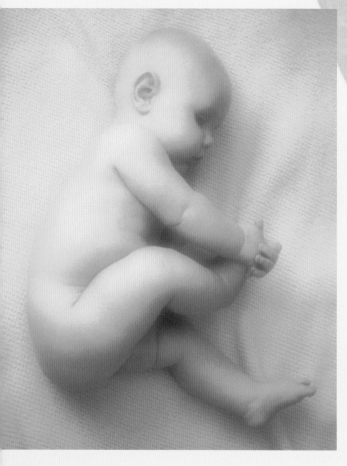

Starting our journey
Below As babies, we develop our base chakra, which is concerned with the kidneys and adrenals. At this point, our first issues of security and trust are addressed.

At the age of 21 our subject moves into her heart center, the fourth chakra, developing issues related to love. She meets someone and falls in love. She wants so much to love and be loved but for some reason it doesn't work out that way. Issues from her earlier life are starting to surface and they are preventing her having the relationship she wants. Unexpressed anger, insecurity, and the need for control start to surface.

Our subject moves into her fifth chakra, the throat, at the age of 28. Now she is dealing with all forms of expression and communication and is at the age where all she has learned is beginning to take form. However, her feelings of insecurity are preventing her from expressing herself fully in all areas of life.

At 35 she moves into the sixth chakra. She is developing her own conscious perception of herself. If, by this stage in her life, she has failed to look at some of her own deep-seated fears and unresolved issues they may surface more strongly.

At 42 she moves into her last cycle, the seventh chakra, and begins to develop understanding of her eternal self. She may yearn to travel to lonely places, embarking on voyages of discovery to find herself. If she does not allow this flowering to occur she will remain in the conflicting cycle of her previous 42 years.

We pass through each stage of development as the relevant issues relating to that chakra are worked on. After the 49th year we will return again to start a new cycle starting with the base chakra.

The wisdom of age
Above During life, we pass through a cycle of seven chakras, ending at age 49. We then begin with a new cycle, starting again at the base chakra.

Lightening the load

Quite often we can ignore and suppress thoughts, feelings, and unresolved issues, choosing to find ways to cope in spite of them. However, this is like carrying excess baggage that simply weighs us down, serving no purpose other than to limit us. If we can identify this excess baggage we may find it is no longer needed—we can continue on our journey with a lighter load.

It is impossible to separate our emotions from our physical body—they are all connected. If we carry unresolved issues on an emotional level, the chakra that was being developed at the time the issue occurred will be affected too. This may mean the flow of vital energy reaching the physical body served by that chakra will be affected as well. Consequently, we find that issues related to any chakra will have an effect on each layer of the three bodies related to it.

Chapter 2

Raising
self-awareness

Chapter 2

"*Native Americans say
life is like
walking backwards:
it is easy to see where
you have been,
not so easy to see where
you are going.*"

Raising self-awareness

WHEN WE LOOK BACK ON OUR LIVES it is easy to see where we have made mistakes, and what we would do differently with hindsight. This is part of the learning process: through the trials and tribulations of life we grow and evolve. This evolution raises our personal awareness so that we can recognize possible pitfalls ahead.

This works very well as long as we remember what has taken place in the past. However, much of our memory has been suppressed and is stored on a cellular or unconscious level. It resides in our energetic fields, affecting us and our daily lives although we can't see how. It is important to start to examine ourselves to find out how we create the pitfalls of our life unconsciously. What unconscious behavior, beliefs, and unresolved emotional issues do we carry around that shape and influence us?

The following pages contain exercises that can help you to develop self-awareness. These exercises ask some of the following questions.

- *Where am I?*
- *What is going on inside me?*
- *What am I carrying with me?*
- *What does the outside world mirror for me?*
- *How have I changed?*

Swimming with fish
Left As the diver is aware of the diversity of life around him, awareness of your surroundings is important in understanding the nature of Reiki.

Exercise 1

CONNECTION TO THE EARTH AND SPIRIT

You need to find an open space in nature to do this exercise.

- To begin, stand with your feet parallel and shoulder width apart. Leave your arms loose beside you and bend your knees a little. Begin to take deep breaths, inhaling through your nose down into your belly, and exhaling through your mouth. Take time to find your natural rhythm—do not force the breath.

- As you breathe become aware of the ground beneath you. What does your connection with the earth feel like? Do you feel grounded, or are you floating above the earth? Imagine the full globe of the earth below you. You are standing on it as it slowly rotates in space. It is your means of survival—your ship as you travel through space. See the image of yourself on the globe. See the beauty of the earth below you.

- Now imagine the sun above you. As you continue to breathe, draw the energy from the sun into your body through the top of your head down into your belly. As you breathe out, imagine the energy traveling down through your base and your feet into the earth like the roots of a tree. Keep breathing in your natural rhythm. Feel yourself supported and grounded on the earth and connected to the sun. Feel the warmth of the sun as it bathes you in its nourishing light. Feel the natural balance between the earth, yourself, and the sun.

- Now imagine the moon below the earth, its silent rhythms pulling the seas of the earth downwards. Feel this pull within yourself. Imagine yourself on the earth, the sun above bathing you in light, the moon below pulling you downwards gently. Experience being a part of the natural rhythms of the earth, the moon, and the sun. Inhale, exhale, and simply feel.

Grounding yourself
Below Imagine yourself standing on top of the earth, and mentally affirm your strong connection with it.

Focusing on pain
Left Internal
scanning allows you
to journey around
your body,
pinpointing any
areas suffering pain
and becoming
aware of emotions
that may be
associated with
that discomfort.

Exercise 2
INTERNAL SCANNING

For this exercise you will need to draw on your powers
of visualization and concentration.

• To begin, find a safe place where you will not be
disturbed. Lie on your back or sit in the lotus position.
Make sure you are comfortable and warm.

• Close your eyes, take a few deep breaths, and relax.

• Now focus your awareness inside yourself. Start at the
feet and work your way up your body slowly. Ask
yourself what you feel. Are you relaxed? What does
your body feel like? As you move through your body
you may find areas of discomfort. Don't try to make

yourself more comfortable by moving around. Instead
give the discomfort your full attention and find out
what it is made of. Any pain in the body will contain
emotions too. Become aware of the feelings contained
within the pain. Allow the pain to be, and if it moves
somewhere else follow it. Try to relax into the pain.

• Continue on through the body. When you find other
painful areas focus on them and again see what
emotions they contain. Journey through your whole
body in this way.

Exercise 3
ETHERIC GAZING

This exercise involves a friend or partner. Before beginning the exercise be sure that you are both willing to engage deeply with each other.

• Sit close together, facing each other either in a chair or on the floor. Try to ensure that you are both sitting in front of a plain wall, as this is less distracting.

• Hold your partner's hands and begin to look into each other's eyes. Question how it feels to be watched and seen. Examine which side of the face you feel more connected to. Which side are you drawn to look at? Allow yourself to connect deeply with the person and examine what they are holding in their face. Are they in pain, and if so where? Is it evident more on one side than the other?

• If you find that the face changes shape, continue with the exercise and observe what changes take place. There may be a darkening of the features, a little like someone turning the lights down, which indicates that you are seeing the person on an etheric level. The features may also change radically: you may see male features on a female face; younger or older faces; or even animal features. Continue with the exercise for about ten minutes and then gently disconnect. Spend time sharing what you saw in each other—you will be surprised at what you have within you.

This exercise can also be done on your own using a mirror. It is a little harder to remain objective but can still be of great benefit.

Face to face
Right Find a quiet, calm setting where you will not be disturbed, and ensure that your partner is willing to devote themself entirely to the exercise.

Exercise 4

OUR FRIENDS AND FAMILY AS A MIRROR

Spend time with your friends and family and really listen to what they say about themselves and how they think about the world.

- *Is it supportive?*
  - *Does it empower them?*
    - *How do you feel when you are with them?*
- *Which areas of your body react to them?*
  - *Does your solar plexus contract?*
    - *Do you get a stomach ache?*
- *Does your throat hurt?*
  - *Do you feel angry, scared, nervous, unable to think?*

- What goes on inside yourself as you interact with these people? Remember that your family and friends are mirrors for you.
- Instead of reacting to the feelings you are experiencing try to observe them. Write your feelings down. Place your hands on the areas of your body that are affected and allow yourself to experience all your feelings.

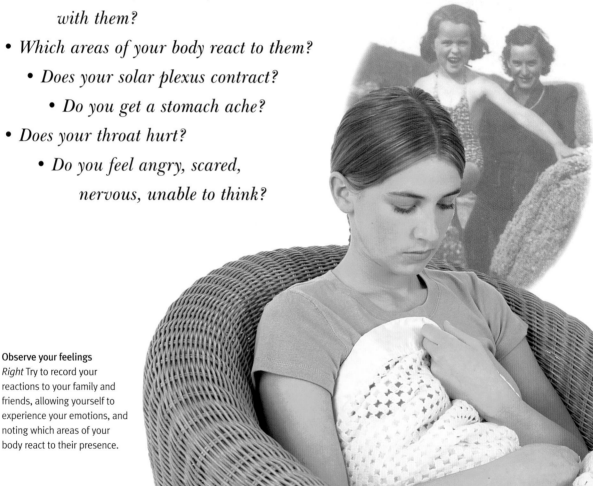

Observe your feelings
Right Try to record your reactions to your family and friends, allowing yourself to experience your emotions, and noting which areas of your body react to their presence.

Exercise 5

INNER CHILD

For this exercise you need to look through the family
album. Find a photograph of yourself as a child that you
are in some way attracted to: maybe you like the way
you are dressed, or the confidence you exuded. Place it
where it can be seen on a regular basis throughout the
day. Carry it with you to and from work. Say good
morning and good night to the child in the photograph.
Begin to build a relationship with the child. Look at who
you were.

Discovering your inner child
Below Use old photographs of
yourself as a child to rediscover
long-forgotten emotions.

- *What do you feel when you look at this photograph?*
  - *What qualities do you resonate with
    when you look at the child?*
    - *What can you learn from this child?*
- *What does this child need?*
  - *What were his/her dreams? Remember that
    this child is still within you.*
- *Did you fulfill those dreams?*

- Ask the child: "Have I turned out OK? What should I
  change?" Draw on the wisdom of the child within to
  teach and guide you. If you are in a situation that
  makes you unhappy, ask your child what they would
  do to remedy matters.

As an individual with a conscious awareness of
who you are, you can start to develop
compassion for others. Recognizing
that each person is doing the best
they can on their chosen path leads
to an acceptance of others, and an
understanding of where you stand on
your own path.

Understanding the male/female split

ONE OF THE MAIN SOURCES OF CONFLICT in the world is between men and women. However, it is often forgotten that we carry both masculine and feminine principles within us, regardless of our physical sex. The photographs below are part of an experiment to demonstrate this fact. Each photograph is a composite made up of a single portrait, the original being duplicated in its mirrored reflection. The photographs are split in two and rejoined with the two left sides of the face together, and the two right sides of the face together. In Reiki the left side of the face represents the female, and the right side the male.

The effects are startling, showing widely different features, expressions, and shapes in the two faces. The two sides reveal the emotional conflicts that are held in the physical features themselves. The imbalance of power between the masculine and feminine within each person is also highlighted.

"All pain, all suffering, is caused by separateness"

BARBARA ANN BRENNAN

Original photograph	**Right side—masculine principle**	**Left side—feminine principle**

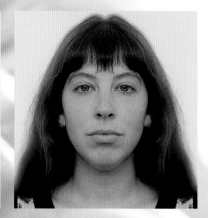 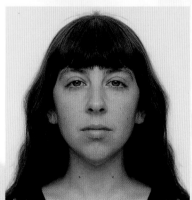

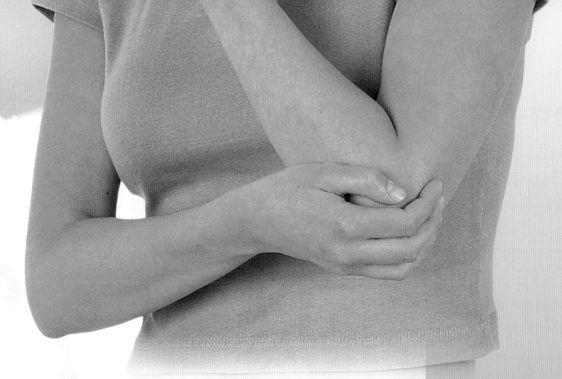

The importance of **touch**

WHEN WE HURT OURSELVES AS CHILDREN it is an instinctive action to put our hand on the pain and "rub it better!". The fact that we are capable of healing forms part of our inner wisdom. Often a person will need nothing more than a gentle touch, a helping hand, or a hug to make them feel better. In this hi-tech world of ours it is easy to forget the healing power of touch.

As you learn to embrace Reiki you will find that your natural tendency to rub things better takes on deep significance.

Masculine and feminine sides
Left Regardless of our gender, the left side of the face represents the female principle of our personality, and the right side, the male. These images, made by duplicating one side of the face in its mirrored reflection, show how the male and female sides of the same person can show completely different characteristics.

The healing touch

I remember a story an elderly lady told me during a flight from Scotland to London. We chatted about my work with Reiki and, to my surprise, she thought it was the most natural thing in the world. She told me that she had been in hospital earlier that year for a small operation and the doctor, realizing she might be a little frightened, had kindly taken her on a tour of the hospital. He had shown her all the life-saving machines that they used in order, I suppose, to instil confidence in her. At the end of the tour, the patient looked at the doctor and said: "Very impressive machines, but where do you do the healing?" He didn't understand what she meant. "Where do you use your hands?" she asked, "Where do you give healing?" The doctor replied they didn't do that in the hospital. The lady was surprised and said, "But doctor, you can't heal without touch."

Chapter 3

First degree Reiki

Chapter 3

> *"I found myself standing at the edge of a cliff looking into an abyss. I knew I had to jump but I was afraid. A hand took mine and a voice gently said 'We can do this together if it will be easier for you.'"*

First degree Reiki

The importance of individuality
Above First degree Reiki is an introspective journey into the self, away from the crowd.

WHEN DR USUI FIRST RECEIVED THE REIKI VISION and empowerment on the top of Mount Kurama it was an enormously powerful experience. The energy was so strong that it rendered him unconscious. At the time, he made the choice to accept the levels of energy that he received. He later decided that, in order for Reiki to be passed on in a safe and responsible way, he would need to develop his teaching in stages. These different levels would be supported with an initiation, or series of initiations, that would facilitate a change in the person's energy field. The idea was that while this initiation would be strong enough to facilitate a transformation it would not knock the student out.

Today we teach Reiki in this way, with three main levels each having a specific set of teachings designed to help the student expand in awareness and develop understanding of energy work at a sensible pace. In today's world of instant gratification, Reiki maintains its tried and tested methods of slowly traveling the path to self-discovery on an energetic level. We are all unique and the journey will be different for everyone.

WHAT IS FIRST DEGREE REIKI?

The first level of Reiki is primarily for the self. It is an experiential journey into awareness of the world of energy, both internal and external. The objective is to discover ways in which the student can clear their personal vessel and become a clear and open channel for the universal life force energy to flow through them. This journey begins by being opened to the flow of this energy through the initiation process.

After the initiation the student must learn to work with the new energy that flows through them. This involves learning to let go of the limitations our minds impose on us and embrace a new world of possibilities. Students are made aware of their own energy, discovering ways in which they can observe themselves objectively. They are given the opportunity to discover a part of themselves that has remained hidden or asleep. First degree Reiki is an opportunity to access the obstacles that prevent people from living in harmony. These blocks may exist emotionally, mentally, or physically, but within the safe and supportive workshop environment we can begin to understand and resolve those inner conflicts. This takes courage: students are asked to face parts of themselves that they have not acknowledged for many years.

The first level is also the introduction to working with energy in a practical way. Students are given set treatments that lay the foundation for future work with energy. They learn how to listen, with their whole body, and establish a connection with their own intuition.

Building trust

The relationship with the teacher is important in helping the student to establish the right time to move on to the next level. It is generally agreed that three months should elapse between first and second degree Reiki, and that a period of a year should be allowed before moving on to the third level.

Initiation
Right Before completing a Reiki course, you will need to undergo an initiation process, forming bonds with your Reiki teacher.

How classes are structured

REIKI IS TAUGHT VERBALLY with very little need to take notes or study. The basic principles behind the teachings are simple, and are explained in an informal way. The history of Reiki is recounted, telling us how this system of healing was discovered and how it came to be in its present form. The classes are usually held over two days.

The first morning is dedicated to group bonding and self-awareness exercises. These exercises make the students aware of how they are feeling, and teach them to concentrate their attention on their internal self through guided meditations. Group sharing gives people the opportunity to tell each other about their own personal journey and what brought them to this point in their lives. It is often encouraging to hear similar stories to your own, as it helps validate your experiences as being real. All these exercises are an important part of the process of helping people to relax and feel less inhibited.

Group bonding
Above Early on in a Reiki course, the students will participate in group discussions and sharing, telling each other about their own personal journeys.

After the first morning the work becomes experiential and is centered around the initiations. These are powerful exchanges of energy from the master to the student, and often the students will require time to sleep as they integrate the experience. Time is put aside for any questions that may need to be asked, or any processing that needs to take place.

The first afternoon is devoted to receiving and giving treatments for the first time. It is often a period of astonishment, as each student becomes aware of their capacity to channel energy. They spend time growing

Each master will structure his or her class to suit their teaching methods. However, all first degree courses should include:

- a verbal introduction giving the history of Reiki methods and practices
- a description of the subtle anatomy of a human being and its effect on our lives
- Initiations (traditionally there are four, although some masters may give two or even just one)
- a description and demonstration of full/foundation treatment with practice
- the self treatment
- the short treatment
- information on how to treat animals, plants, and your environment
- what to do in emergencies
- and, importantly, lots of hugs

accustomed to the strange new sensations passing through their hands and bodies, as they learn to recognize what different energies feel like.

The second day is dedicated to teaching the self treatment, the short treatment, and discussing ways in which Reiki can be used on a daily basis to enhance your life. The positions of the full treatment are covered and time is given to allow any personal transformations within the group to take place.

Initiation
Left The energy channels are opened through the initiation, a powerful yet simple process that connects us to Reiki.

Initiations

THERE ARE FOUR INITIATIONS IN THE FIRST DEGREE REIKI COURSE, based on the original teachings of Dr Usui. They are designed to open up our ability to channel the healing energy of the universe more effectively. Every person is connected, whether conscious of it or not, to this universal energy. This connection is enhanced through the Reiki initiation process. In addition, it is a guarantee of the lineage or pathway that the energy follows before flowing through you. It forms the foundation of our connection to this energy and the specific spiritual guidance that accompanies it.

Though deeply profound and moving, the process of initiation is very simple. The master acts as a channel through which the guides and energy work. The guides of the person receiving the initiation are also present. The master follows a series of movements, placing symbols into key energy points in the student. These serve to anchor the Reiki vibration into their physical, mental, emotional, and spiritual bodies.

The master begins with the crown center then, in a flowing sequence, will work through the third eye, the heart, and the root centers to anchor the energy. The master will then continue through the hand chakras, to

> **"We are all like pendulums: start a bunch of pendulums swinging randomly and come back a while later to find that they are all swinging in resonance. Given a little help and encouragement, we will all move towards resonance with each other."**
>
> DANAAN PARRY

allow the healing energy to flow from the heart through the hands. Finally, the student is grounded by connecting the energy to the two chakras in the feet. This initiation is very powerful and, once anchored, remains for life. After the initiation the student will normally feel strong rushes of heat through their main vertical power channel down the spine. Their hands will become very hot as they are charged with the energy.

The initiations are seen as healings in themselves. They introduce such a powerful love vibration into the student's field of energy that any lower vibrational thought patterns and emotions start to rise up into the consciousness. Because of this, a period of integration is required, said to be approximately 21 days. This three-week period is often accompanied by a fair amount of turbulence as old feelings, memories, and experiences begin to surface. During this time of transformation it is important to apply the self-healing techniques learnt during the first degree course.

Healing hands
Above Like a burning candle, the Reiki that rushes into a student after initiation can take the form of heat and energy.

Foundation treatment

Relaxation
Above At the beginning of the session, allow the client to close their eyes and relax into it.

PREPARATION

A session begins before the person arrives and ends after they have left. It is important that you spend some time preparing yourself and the space around you for what you are about to do.

- *Burn some incense to clear any stagnant energy that may exist.*
- *Ensure the room temperature is comfortable.*
- *Play gentle music to help the client relax.*
- *Have some fresh drinking water to hand, as energy work tends to dehydrate both you and your client.*
- *Use fresh, clean linen and keep a warm blanket to cover the client if they get cold.*
- *Unplug all telephones and make sure you will not be disturbed.*

Invocation
Above Invoke your guides and angels and feel the presence of the energy as it surrounds you.

Once everything is ready sit still and focus in on yourself. Take a few moments to scan through your field and take note of how you are feeling. It is important to identify and own the feelings that are yours so you do not project them onto your client. In an ideal world you will be clear of any personal issues, but this is seldom the case. Use the invocation prayer to invite your guides and helpers into the room with you. Use their energy to give yourself ten minutes of Reiki into the heart center and solar plexus. This will ensure you are centered.

FIRST IMPRESSIONS

It is important to record your first impressions when you meet the client. What is their body language telling you? Perhaps they have their arms crossed tightly over their solar plexus to protect themself. This could mean that they have an issue related to that chakra.

Introduce yourself and, if it is their first time receiving Reiki, explain a little about its background and methods. Chat to them and make them feel relaxed.

"I AM THE PRESENCE calling on the universal life force energy to come from source through Christ with love, light, and wisdom. I ask for my guides and angels to be with me to guide and protect me. I ask for the Reiki masters past and present to be with me, in particular the grand masters Dr Usui, Dr Hayashi, and Hawayo Takata. I ask that they ensure all that takes place is of the very highest good for all concerned. I am the love of God, I am the light of God, I am the healing power of God. I am. I am. I am."

Invocation

ONE OF THE UNIQUE ASPECTS OF WORKING WITH REIKI is the connection to the lineage of Dr Usui. Through the initiation process we have a specific pathway that forms our connection to the Reiki. As we work with the energy we become part of this lineage and can call on that lineage to assist us in our work.

The power of invocation and prayer is an important part of the healing process, helping us to verbally state our intention for the healing we are about to do. By calling on our guides, the Reiki masters, and the universal energy we are empowering and affirming our intention. This ensures that we are creating a safe environment for ourselves and those who come to us, and that we will be protected at all times. It is also an important part of surrendering to the free flow of energy through us, helping us to remember our connection to the universe, and the origins of the energy we are using.

Above is a powerful invocation that can be used for this purpose. It can also be repeated as you begin the healing session. Of course, it is not always possible to prepare yourself in this way. If you are working in an emergency or in a public place it is advisable to invoke your helpers silently as you are working.

If you feel a connection to a particular guide, angel, or ascended master you can include them in your invocation.

The Reiki family

I would describe my experience of invocation as like having a family that I am connected to through the initiation process. When I call on the energy, the family comes too.

Full body treatment

SMOOTHING THE AURA

Before treatment begins, smooth the aura by gently stroking your hands from the head to the feet in a circular motion. This helps to settle the client's energy in preparation for the healing session, and also seals the energies in at the end of a session. By gently stroking your hands through the aura, approximately 8 in (20cm) from the body, you are able to feel any imbalances in the client's energy centers. I suggest the use of aurosoma pomanders and quintessence for this technique.

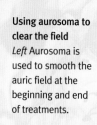

Using aurosoma to clear the field
Left Aurosoma is used to smooth the auric field at the beginning and end of treatments.

Tuning in
Above Take a few moments to center yourself and connect with the Reiki energy before entering the patient's energy field.

Smoothing the aura
Left Gently stroke your hand through the aura to feel for energy imbalances.

FRONT POSITIONS

1 **Over the forehead, eyes, and cheeks**
For the treatment of eye problems, sinuses, colds, allergies, nerves in the brain, pituitary and pineal gland. Effective in balancing the pineal gland, which is the center of hormonal regulation. This position helps the client to relax, and stimulates and balances the sixth Chakra.

2 **To the sides of the temples** For the treatment of optic nerves, and effective in balancing the right and left sides of the brain. This position is very relaxing for clients suffering from stress.

3 **Over the ears** Treats many organs, via the acupuncture points in this area, including the heart, intestines, kidneys, lungs, stomach, liver, and gall bladder.

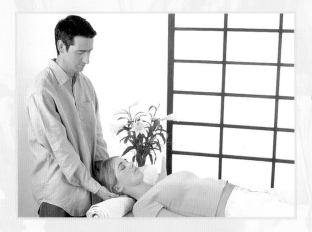

4 **Back of the head** fingertips on medulla oblongata, which is connected to the third eye. For eyes, vision, headaches, nose bleeds, stroke, and pineal gland. Memory bank for all childhood and past life emotional trauma.

5 **Throat** Relates to the fifth chakra. For sore throat, flu, high blood pressure, anger, the thyroid gland, frustration, and problems with expression. The throat chakra effects communication and creativity.

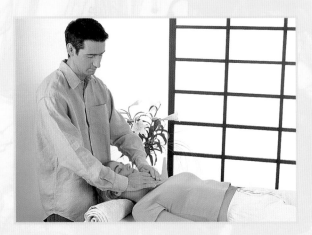

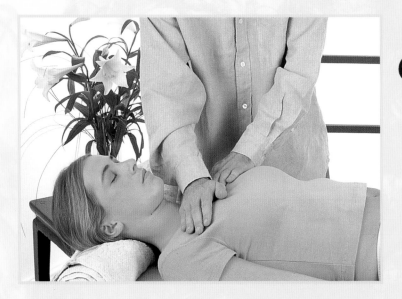

6 **Thymus gland/upper chest** This is where we feel fear, panic, stress, and a whole range of emotions. It is known as the survival spot, and affects energy levels. People often feel a sense of suffocation in this area when their heart chakra closes, which reveals problems with relating to others.

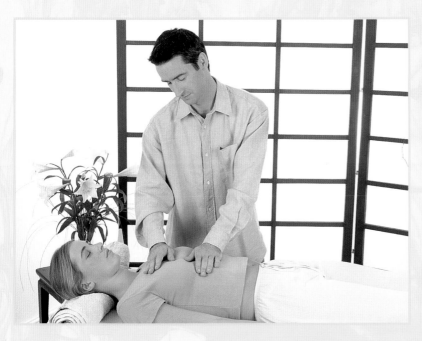

7 **Solar plexus and heart** Relate to the third and fourth chakras. Treat the solar plexus for digestive problems and patterns of behavior, and the heart for emotional blockages, circulation, stress, and heart problems. The fourth chakra affects our ability to love ourselves and others on all levels.

8 **Liver and spleen** For the treatment of toxification on all levels, suppression of anger, bitterness, sadness, and depression. This area also includes the gall bladder and the pancreas.

9 **Hara/belly** Again, deals with the suppression of all issues relating to power. This area also includes the intestines and duodenum.

10 **Hara/belly** This position can be extended to the sides of the body to include the outer hara.

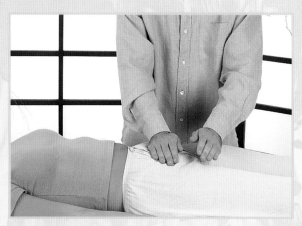

11 **Pubic bone** Relates to the second chakra. For the treatment of sexual organs, prostrate, bladder, ovaries, urethra, and appendix. Deals with issues concerned with self-worth and creativity, as well as physical, mental, emotional, or spiritual problems due to a misalignment with Mother Earth. In extreme cases, this is the area where suppressed sexual issues, such as rape, abuse, or incest, are stored.

CHAKRA HARMONIZING

Place your hands above the body at the first and sixth chakras, then move your hands together and place them over the second and fifth chakras, before moving on to the third and fourth chakras. Hold each position for one or two minutes, or until you feel the need to move on.

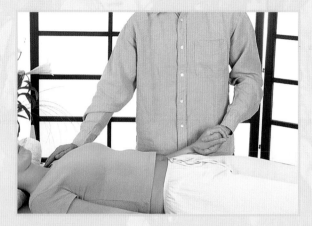

12 **Shoulders and arms** Connects the main heart and colon meridians, and helps to comfort the client.

13 **Hips and knees** For the treatment of sciatica, arthritis, and joint pains in general. This is another emotional storage area. Stiffness in this region can suggest problems with changing beliefs and moving forward with life.

14 **Feet** These contain meridian points that relate to all parts of the body. Holding the feet helps to ground the client.

BACK POSITIONS

1 **Shoulders** This position helps to relieve any stress that has built up in this area. The shoulders are where we carry the burdens of other people's expectations of us; our mother's on the left, our father's on the right.

2 **Upper back/lung** Relates to the heart, so the ailments for Front Position 7 apply. This position is also beneficial to clients suffering from bronchial problems.

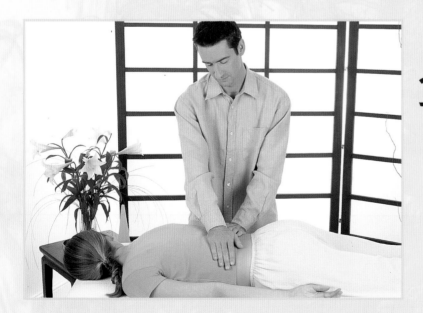

3 **Middle back/lung** Relates to the solar plexus, spleen, liver, pancreas, stomach, and gall bladder.

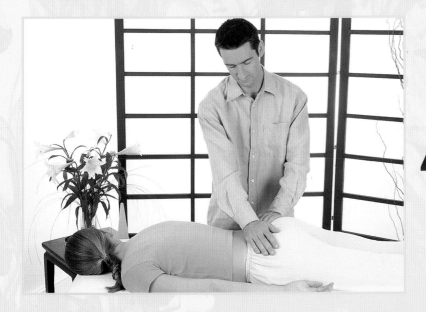

4 **Lower back** Relates to the second chakra, so the ailments for Front Position 11 apply. Also for the treatment of sciatica. This is another emotional storage area.

5 **Buttocks** Again, relates to the second chakra. This is an emotional storage area relating to our childhood. Issues such as sexual abuse are often found here.

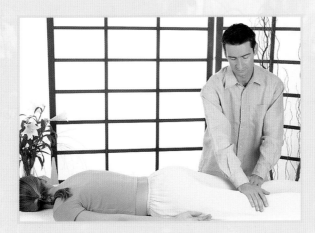

6 **Back of the knees** This covers two minor chakras at the back of the knees and helps to ground energy. The knees are symbolic of our fear in moving forward in life.

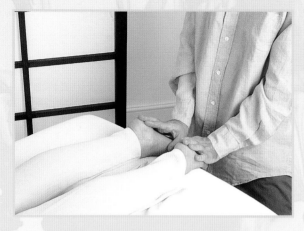

7 **Feet** This position grounds the client, balancing the whole treatment and grounding energies into the minor feet chakras.

8 **Coccyx and the top of the spine/seventh vertebrae** This position helps energy to run through the spine and remove any blockages that may exist.

9 **Heart and solar plexus** This final position closes the session and places energy into the heart and solar plexus so that the client will feel centered and empowered.

CHECKLIST FOR FULL TREATMENT

1 Spend some time preparing your Reiki space with sage or incense to help clear the energy in the room.

2 If you are using a table, prepare it with a covering of paper towel or clean linen.

3 Take a few moments to sit quietly and give yourself Reiki, concentrating on your heart and solar plexus areas to clear your own energy.

4 Your first impressions of your client are important. Often people will not disclose how they really feel, so it is important to trust your own observations. Something that appears quite irrelevant could be the key to the healing.

5 We are not doctors and it is important to remind the client that we cannot predict the outcome of a healing or work on specific areas. We can only ask for the best for our client, and offer the healing as a complementary therapy. Explain this to the client, and tell them a little of what you will be doing and what they can expect. Make them as comfortable as possible.

6 Begin by scanning the client with your hands and make a mental note of any areas that seem out of balance to you.

7 Having begun the healing show respect for the client's well-being at all times. Try to stay present and focused, and allow yourself to be guided.

8 Encourage any emotional releases and reassure your client that it is OK for them to feel this way.

9 Seal the aura with gentle strokes in an anti-clockwise direction around the full length of the body. Tell the client that they have five minutes to bring themselves round. Wash your hands and fetch them some drinking water.

10 Help your client off the table and check how they feel.

11 Once the client has left prepare the room again. Give thanks to your guides and angels for the help you received and take a break in the fresh air to ground yourself.

12 Check your energy for anything that you feel you may have taken on board and clear it with Reiki before continuing with other treatments.

Short treatment

THE SHORT TREATMENT has been specifically designed for working in on-site situations where there are time restraints. It can be used in many different situations and you do not need to invest in a proper portable massage table.

Use a chair with an open back, to enable the hands to make direct contact with both sides of the person. The positions have been developed to maximize the available time while still concentrating on the key energetic points of the body. As with the full treatment, begin at the head and work your way down through the main vertical channel of the chakras. The front and back of the chakras are worked at the same time, treating both sides of the same chakra as a whole.

It is important that the client is comfortable, and that they take off their shoes and keep their feet firmly placed on the ground. Try to make sure they are sitting upright to prevent any blockage to the flow of energy forming along the spine. Key aspects of the full treatment still apply to the short treatment. For example, the client needs to be treated with the same care and attention, they must be in a safe place where there are no distractions, and you need to be sure you will not be disturbed. These factors will allow the client to relax into the treatment and benefit fully from the healing.

1 Stand at the side and place one hand in front of the third eye and the other to the back of the head. Hold for three minutes. The hand at the front can be held 2–3 in (5–7 1/2 cm) from the forehead, or placed directly over it.

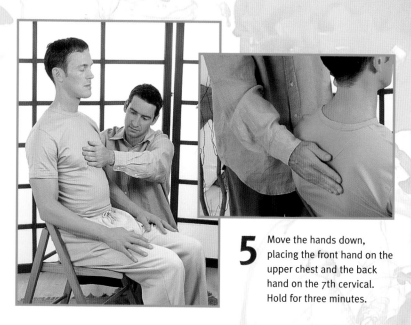

5 Move the hands down, placing the front hand on the upper chest and the back hand on the 7th cervical. Hold for three minutes.

6 Place the front hand on the heart, with the back hand mirroring it by working on the rear aspect of the heart chakra. Hold for three minutes.

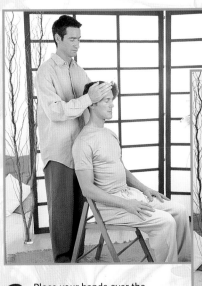

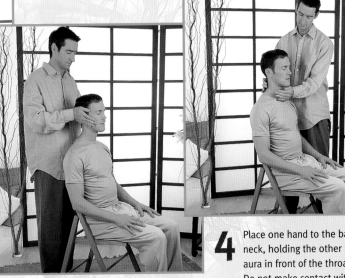

2 Place your hands over the temples, fingers pointing forwards. Hands can be held in the aura or kept in contact with the body.

3 Gently place your hand over the ears. The palms of your hands should be cupped over the ears, with fingers pointing along the jaw bone. Hold for three minutes.

4 Place one hand to the back of the neck, holding the other in the aura in front of the throat chakra. Do not make contact with the throat, as this can feel invasive and uncomfortable. Hold for three minutes.

7 Place the front hand on the solar plexus, with the back hand again mirroring this action on the middle of the back. Hold for three minutes.

8 Move to the front of the body and kneel down. Place both hands together over each hip. Hold for three minutes.

9 Place both hands over the tops of the feet, helping to ground the person to end the treatment. Again, hold for three minutes.

Self treatment

SELF TREATMENT IS THE MAINSTAY of your personal relationship to the Reiki energy. It helps you to maintain your connection, to deepen your relationship to the energy, and to work on a continual basis to clear your own vessel. This process never stops, and it is advisable to maintain a discipline of working with the self treatment once a day.

The basis of the treatment mirrors that of the short treatment and foundation treatment, beginning with the head positions and working through the main energy centers down the body to the feet. Once you have learned one treatment you will find that others come easily.

During your first encounters with Reiki you will be concerned with your own transformation and healing. However, you will find that as you go further in your work with energy, and start to work on others, this self treatment plays an important role in maintaining your own energy and keeping yourself clear. With the help of self treatment you can recognize any changes taking place in your own energy field and clear it out easily and efficiently. By maintaining high levels of Ki in your etheric field you help yourself stay healthy and improve your immunity to disease. So you may find that if you come into contact with the flu virus, you can clear away the symptoms energetically from your field of energy. In doing this you may not need to take on the actual physical symptoms.

One of the Reiki master's commitments is to work every day with the self treatment to keep themselves clear and open. It is important to remember that the treatment forms a foundation that should be refered to whenever you work. However, if you have areas outside this foundation that need to receive healing do not feel bound by the format of the treatment. In other words, place your hands wherever you feel pain.

The self treatment is a beautiful way to nurture yourself on all levels. Whatever is going on in your life, this simple and effective technique can provide you with support.

Invocation

Above As with other forms of Reiki treatment, begin with an invocation to the Reiki masters and the universal Reiki energy (see page 47).

Penetrating heat

On the day after a first degree Reiki course one of my students told me that she had compared the heat of her hands to that from a hot water bottle. She had been amazed at how the heat from her hands had penetrated deeply into her body, whereas the hot water bottle heated only the surface.

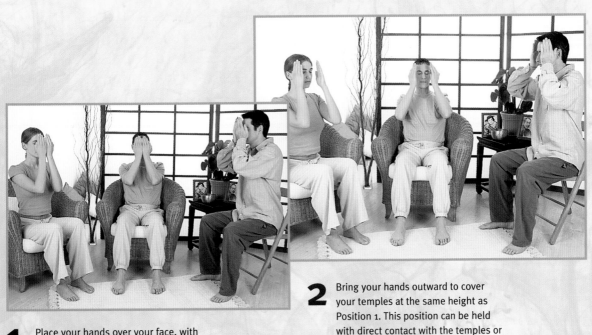

1 Place your hands over your face, with the palms over your eyes and your fingers pointing upwards towards your hairline. Keep your fingers and thumbs closed and relax. Hold this position for three minutes.

2 Bring your hands outward to cover your temples at the same height as Position 1. This position can be held with direct contact with the temples or about 3 in (7 ½ cm) away.

3 Cover both ears with your palms, keeping your fingers together. This is a powerful position to bring a sense of balance to the left and right sides of the brain and body.

4 Place both hands behind the head, in whichever way is most comfortable. This area is connected to the third eye and is regarded as the memory bank for stored emotional memories.

5 Place one hand at the back of your neck and the other over your throat, working on both sides of the throat chakra at the same time.

6 Place one hand on your heart and the other on your solar plexus chakra. This position can be used at any time during the day to help center you.

9 Place the hands in a V shape from your hip bone, pointing downward and covering the pubic bone so that your fingertips touch. For women, this is very helpful for the alleviation of pain during the menstrual cycle.

10 Place your hands behind your back, covering the area below your ribs. Your fingers will automatically point inwards to touch each other. This area focuses on the kidneys and adrenals.

7 Place two hands horizontally just under the breast, fingers pointing toward each other. This is an important emotional storage point, where we suppress anger.

8 Place one hand on top of the other, covering the entire digestive area. Your hands should face in opposite directions and sit above and below the belly button.

11 Place your hands over both knees, fingers pointing downward. The knees are areas where we hold resistance and fear about moving forward in our lives.

12 Finally, hold each foot for a few minutes. This action helps you to ground yourself, and treats the numerous meridian points on the feet and toes.

Chapter 4

Second degree Reiki

Chapter 4

Second degree Reiki
Involving a deeper commitment to the principles of Reiki, taking you to a new level of understanding.

How classes are structured
What to expect when attending a second degree Reiki course.

A deeper understanding of Energetics
All of nature is interconnected, so a global understanding of Reiki is essential.

The three golden keys
The secret symbols that unlock the power of healing, discussed in detail.

Distant healing
Healing energy can be sent across distances using Reiki. You can even "heal" an event in your future.

The power of intention
How to ensure the Reiki energy is used as purely as possible.

Developing your empathic abilities
Exercises and case studies to help you empathize on a deeper level.

Energy blockages
Advanced techniques to clear energy blockages using Reiki.

> *"Illness is some form of external searching. Health is inner peace."*
>
> COURSE OF MIRACLES

Second degree
Reiki

AFTER THE INTEGRATION PERIOD OF 21 DAYS that follows the first degree initiations students have usually decided whether they wish to continue to gain more skills and understanding in Reiki. In traditional Reiki a period of three months is required before the student is able to continue onto second degree. This is to allow all the changes that take place in the student's field after the first level time to rebalance and be fully integrated. However, we are all different and this period is, therefore, merely a guideline. Normally, the student and master will determine the correct time to move on to the second degree level.

The intention of the second degree is to make a deeper commitment to healing both ourselves and others. Usually it is those people who have healed their

A deeper commitment
Left To progress to second degree Reiki, you must show a deeper level of commitment, as in marriage, to healing yourself and others.

Rose
Above As you go on to study second degree Reiki, your understanding and healing ability will develop and blossom like a rose.

own lives, through awareness and commitment to change, that are the best guides for others to do the same. It is important that those people who go on to second degree Reiki have gone some way towards understanding their own process, and have understood the help Reiki has given them in that process. They must see the journey forward as a means of self-development, as well as a route to help others.

During the second degree course the student is introduced to the three key Reiki symbols, as shown to Dr Usui on Mount Kurama in Japan. Each symbol has a specific function, and during the two-day course the student will learn the importance these symbols have in future healing work. Issues held on emotional and mental levels can rise up into our consciousness and, through the skills we learn on the course, we are able to work on these at a far deeper level. Second degree introduces the student to powerful new ideas, making them more aware of the connection to all that is. We begin to understand that the past, present, and future can all be accessed in the now.

We learn to use that connection to heal our present situation by sending healing to wherever the issues originally occurred. This opens our awareness as we learn to connect to our own childhood, for example, or to people from our past who still affect us in some way. We are introduced to the ability to send energy across distance, learning that we are not restricted by space. We can connect to people, places, or situations and support them through the healing power of Reiki, wherever they may be. This then introduces group work and the power of sending energy to places of crisis in the world. Through exercises we learn to focus our intention and, through the unlimited nature of Reiki, send love to wherever it is needed.

How classes are structured

THE SECOND DEGREE COURSE is usually held over two days, during which time students are introduced to the three second level symbols. The meaning of each symbol is discussed in turn, the students being invited to give their own perceptions of each symbol. I am always amazed at the accuracy of their perceptions, and encourage these to be shared before giving the traditional view.

After the symbols have been shown they are empowered through an initiation. Only one initiation is given on the second degree course. This initiation is designed to empower the symbols given to us, the belief being that without the initiation the symbols have little power or meaning. This is the reason why some masters have felt justified in publishing the symbols in books or on the Internet. The traditional view is that the symbols are secret and should remain so.

The course is structured around the symbols, with exercises given to demonstrate how they work. These involve the emotional and mental healing technique and distant healing techniques. I also devote time to

Distant healing
Right Photographs of loved ones can be used for distant healing: Reiki can be sent over distance to friends and family.

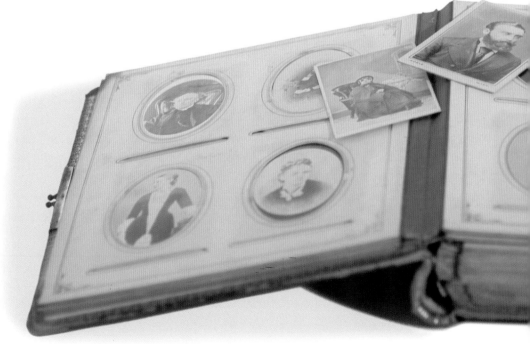

group sharing of each individual's experiences since completing the first level. It often helps to consolidate each person's experience when they hear of other people's journeys.

I ask the group to bring in photographs of themselves as children, as well as photographs of friends or family. These are used in distant healing exercises connecting to the person in the photograph and sending healing to them.

I also devote time to increasing the students' awareness of their own energy field through self awareness exercises, thus increasing their empathic abilities.

Students learn the importance of setting up the healing space, how to clear a space of negative energies in preparation for healing, and how to prepare themselves for a treatment. At the end of a treatment they are taught how to clear their energy.

By the end of the course the students feel confident in their knowledge of the symbols and how they are to be used. They should feel confident in their ability to hold a space for another to receive Reiki and be able to cope with any emotional releases that may occur as they work. They will have a growing trust in their intuitive abilities and in the energies they are working with. They will also have a deeper commitment to their own personal growth and transformation with the help of Reiki.

A second degree Reiki course should include:
- the three symbols and their uses
- mental and emotional healing
- group healing
- distant healing work
- lots of group hugs.

As you let yourself be healed, you see all those around you, or who cross your mind, or whom you touch, or those that seem to have no contact with you, healed along with you . . . you are never healed alone.

COURSE OF MIRACLES

A deeper understanding of energetics

AS WE BEGIN TO USE THE REIKI TREATMENTS we have learned, it is interesting to observe the range of people we attract. Nothing ever happens by chance, so it is often helpful for us to note the issues carried by those people we treat. Often they will reflect issues that we still hold ourselves and are working on, or issues we have resolved in our own lives. This places us in the perfect position to help them with their own process as we draw from our own experience.

I have often seen that people are brought together who carry very similar issues. Either they share similar experiences and so are able to empathize with each other, or they operate from a place of polarity observing how their own behaviour may be affecting another.

When a person releases a long-held issue it can begin a chain reaction within the group. Others will also release similar issues that they hold, or observe the suffering their actions may have caused in others. It is as if the group has tuned into a particular frequency that represents an issue and anyone who carries that issue in their field begins to be affected.

If this can take place within a group then it also holds true that as we begin healing issues individually, the effect of that healing may be felt globally by everyone who holds that issue within their field. The idea that a butterfly flapping its wings can cause a tidal wave on the other side of the world follows the same principle. This is a powerful concept and one that I encourage my students to embrace. If we accept that we are all one then any shift taking place anywhere affects us all, no matter how small that shift may be.

I saw this principle take effect in the most intense way when Princess Diana and Mother Teresa died. These two incidents had a profound effect across the world, uniting East and West in their collective grief. Of course, these were significant events, but they demonstrate how interconnected we all are. Many people sensitive to energy changes have remarked that this was the final gift from these two remarkable women: to unite humanity for a moment and show the power of love and the potential of a human race that is centered in the heart chakra.

Connections
Above All of nature is interconnected: even the smallest events form links and chains that reverberate across the world. In the same way, within any group of people, many of them may be dealing with the same issues as each other, setting off chain reactions within the group. A global approach to Reiki healing is helpful in diagnosing and solving these issues.

The three golden keys

- *Power*
- *Emotional Mental*
- *Distant Healing*

WHEN I TALK OF THE THREE SYMBOLS given in second degree Reiki I refer to them as the three golden keys, because each gives us access through a different doorway. These doorways are: the doorway into the universal energy; the doorway between the physical, emotional, and mental bodies; and the doorway outside of time and space. These symbols then act like keys to unlock the doors that separate us from experiences that are either suppressed or simply out of our range of awareness. Each symbol is accompanied by a mantra which, like the symbol itself, is traditionally only disclosed to students of second level Reiki and must be committed to memory.

One aspect of the symbols which students often question is the variation in how they are drawn between masters. This occurs in the same way as it would if somebody was to write something down on a piece of paper and others were to copy it. Each would copy it in a slightly different way. Imagine then that the symbols have been passed on in this way for over 100 years. It is amazing that they remain as similar as they are. The power is inherent within the symbol in the form that it is presented to you, so this is how you should continue to draw it.

Part of traditional teaching involves a ritual burning of the symbols once they have been learnt. This is designed to return the symbols to spirit and ensures they are always kept secret. This ritual is very powerful and is often the moment when students become fully aware of the symbol's vibration. More sensitive students can feel the change in the room as this takes place.

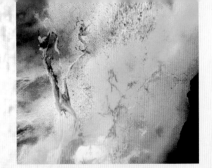

SYMBOL *Power*

ELEMENT *Earth*

MANTRA TRANSLATION *Super Void Light*

THE FIRST OF THE GOLDEN KEYS is the key to the doorway of universal energy. Before, we would knock on the door and it would be opened from the other side. Now we have the key to that door and we can open it whenever we choose. It is called the power symbol because it gives power to all that we do. It increases the power of our work by increasing the energy available to us.

The symbol is made up of three parts: the spiritual plane; the journey from spirit to earth that the soul makes; and the spirals of life that are found in every cell in creation. The three parts resemble a musical note and, just as our cells are sung into being through the specific tone their DNA makes, so this symbol could represent all the tones in all creation. The power symbol is connected to the element of earth and feels very grounded when used. When it is drawn by the practitioner it is experienced as a flush of heat through the body, with a pulse of energy in the palms of the hands.

We use this symbol to increase the flow of energy to particular areas during a healing. It is often used to begin a healing session, the practitioner drawing the symbol into each palm of his or her own hands to help connect themselves to the healing energy. It is helpful to draw this symbol into each chakra as you move down through the treatment to increase the flow of energy reaching them. The power symbol can be used at any time throughout a healing and in any area that requires additional energy.

This symbol is also used to clear and prepare a healing space by drawing it into the four corners of the room. This seals the room and clears any low vibration energy that may be present. It also helps to anchor the vibration of love and light in the room.

The power symbol is the carrier of all the other symbols, so whenever we use another symbol we always seal it with the power symbol. It is also a symbol for protection on all levels—physical, emotional, mental, and spiritual.

The power symbol can protect us physically and can also be used to protect our belongings, which we can do by simply drawing the symbol onto the object. We can use this symbol for protection during emotional conflicts by visualising the symbol and mentally sending it to whichever chakra or area of the body is engaged in the conflict.

A gift of love

We can use this symbol whenever we wish to seal an intention. For example, if we are sending a letter to somebody we can place energy into the letter and then seal it with the symbol. When the person receives the letter they will also receive the energy. I experienced this two years ago, when a dear friend of mine was in hospital and had written asking me for support. He was a little sceptical of Reiki at the time but was reaching out to me. I wrote him a letter and carried it wherever I went for a day, and when I had a moment I would place Reiki into it. Finally, I drew the power symbol onto it. My friend said that on opening the letter he had seen me surrounded in golden light. The experience had moved him to tears. He later told me that this marked the turnaround in his own personal healing.

His girlfriend had been present when he opened the letter and, months later, she asked me what was inside it. "Love," I said.

You can use the symbol to bless any object that you wish, infusing the vibration of love into it.

SYMBOL *Emotional Mental*

ELEMENT *Water*

MANTRA TRANSLATION *Nature, Habit*

THE SECOND GOLDEN KEY is to the doorway between the physical, emotional, and mental bodies. The symbol is comprised of left and right, representing the masculine and feminine aspects, and comes from Sanskrit, symbolizing the Tibetan Goddess of Mercy. It is connected to the element of water, which helps us to understand its action. Water is deeply connected to our emotional nature, working to restore harmony between the physical, mental, and emotional bodies. It helps us to remember emotional memory, beliefs, or trauma that may be held in the physical body and the field around it. This memory will often relate specifically to a period of our lives where discomfort or trauma was experienced which, though suppressed, still affects our lives in unconscious ways. It enables us to release these emotions or traumas.

In addition, this symbol can also help to resolve present-day conflicts or emotional trauma that may occur as a result of an accident or surgery. It works on the mental body in releasing old patterns that no longer serve and may be standing in the way of healing on other levels. It can be drawn into an area that is detected as "out of balance" at any time during healing.

A specific healing technique, unique to this symbol, is called emotional and mental healing. This is a simple use of the symbols drawn specifically into the third eye. This healing is deeply profound and can be the key to unlocking dreams for the future, as well as issues from the past.

Unlocking the memory

I experienced an example of the emotional mental symbol's power in a recent second degree workshop. I had introduced the symbol and asked the students to sit with it and see what they felt. Within seconds one of the students started to cry and said she couldn't continue looking at the symbol. She had seen images from her childhood that she had forgotten: the symbol had literally unlocked the memory and brought it into her awareness again. This is a powerful way to resolve issues. In her case, she went on to express the anger she felt and has gone some way towards healing that particular emotional scar.

SYMBOL *Distant Healing*

ELEMENT *Sun*

MANTRA TRANSLATION *True Men Need Pure Hearts*

THE THIRD OF THE GOLDEN KEYS is to the doorway that takes us outside of time and space. It symbolizes the universal part of us that can reach out to all that is. With the help of our intention it connects us to a person, place, or situation etherically allowing the Reiki to flow from source to wherever it is needed. It is specifically used in group work where it is the group's intention to send energy to situations, people, or places that require healing. There are many Reiki groups throughout the world that co-ordinate their efforts and together shine light on an area of the planet that needs help.

This symbol is primarily used to send Reiki over distance. It can be used to connect to someone who is too far away to arrange a normal session but requires healing to help them through a difficult period. It can also be used to send energy to a situation or event that requires healing on some level, such as peace talks between nations or conflicts on a national scale that have the potential for war.

Most people find this concept acceptable in terms of their own belief system. They might have had the experience of thinking about someone moments before that person calls them on the phone. Or they may have felt uneasy when thinking of a friend only to discover that the person has been going through trauma of some kind. The idea, therefore, that we can connect to another and send healing energy to them is within the realms of possibility for most people.

The interesting part comes when we talk about this symbol's other uses. Through the use of this key we are able to go outside of time and connect to any place we choose for the purpose of healing a situation. For example, if we are able to go back to a point in time when current issues and pain were created, then we are able to trigger the release of the issue in the present.

During the second degree course I guide the group through a healing that involves going back to a period in childhood. By using the symbol we send energy to that time to release any issues that are held. It is powerful to watch the shift taking place within people as they find themselves releasing issues at a very deep level.

Energy over distance

I have had many experiences of distant healing. Most have simply involved experiencing a warm cloak of energy descend on me as other Reiki practitioners have sent energy to me. I was to do a presentation recently in Italy and some of my students had come by the house beforehand to talk. I felt unusually nervous so went upstairs to spend some time preparing myself. While I was in meditation I felt a huge wave of energy sweep over me and instantly I felt calm and at ease. I went downstairs to find my students in a circle holding hands. They felt me coming in and opened their eyes. "We were just sending energy to you," they said. "I know," I replied, "I have just received it."

Distant healing

SENDING DISTANT HEALING

When sending distant healing it is important to create a space that enables you to open up to Reiki without fear of being disturbed. If possible, the recipient should be aware of the time you will connect to them so they too can utilize the energy to the best effect. Go through the procedure of invocation and preparing your space as if you were doing a session one on one. I will usually combine a self-treatment with distant work, working first on myself and then spending time to connect with others. This way I am focused and centered in the energy and can be of more benefit to others.

Light a candle and sit facing it. If you have a photograph of the person place it near the candle so that you can focus on them. If not, you can visualize them or write their name on a piece of paper and place it next to the candle. An object belonging to the person can also be used to form a connection. If you have the second level symbols then use the sequence your master taught you.

If you prefer, you may try this sequence which is very powerful and is the sequence I teach:

- *name of person three times*
- *power symbol three times*
- *mental, emotional symbol three times*
- *power symbol three times*
- *distant symbol three times*
- *power symbol three times*

Once drawn or visualized, take a breath and blow through the palms of your hands, visualizing the person or simply focusing on the photograph or object you have in front of you. You then simply hold your attention on the person for approximately 10 minutes. With practice you will be able to feel the emotional space the person is in and even the physical symptoms they are carrying. The simplest way to do this is by working through the chakras one at a time and registering how your own chakras respond.

Using the same procedure, you may send distant healing in the same way to an event in your future, such as an important exam or interview. Instead of a person, focus on the event that you wish to send energy to.

Using photographs
Above To help you visualize and focus on the intended recipient of your distant healing, look closely at a photograph of them before sending the Reiki.

Blowing the energy
Below Blow the energy through your palm chakras, holding an image of the recipient in your mind throughout.

"We may be brothers after all. We shall see..."

CHIEF SEATTLE

WORKING AS A GROUP

When we work with a group our power is multiplied by the number of
people in the group. Many different projects can be chosen by the group
and these should be clarified before beginning. The group should sit in a
circle facing each other with a candle placed in the middle. Each person in
the group can nominate an individual and provide a photograph or object
of that individual, placing it into the center of the circle. If the group decides
to work on a political issue or a recent disaster, such as an earthquake, then
that intention is placed into the circle. It helps to have an individual
nominated to focalize the group, taking them into the healing and then
bringing them out again. The same procedure is followed as before.
All members of the group draw the sequence of symbols and together blow
the energy into the center of the circle. Hold the focus for 10 minutes and
then gently bring the focus back to the room.

Afterwards the group can share their individual experiences.

Personal objects
Above Use a personal object to connect you
to the time, place, or person you wish to
send healing to.

BEAMING ENERGY

The sequence of symbols I have given on page 76 can be used to beam energy at whatever you choose. A useful group healing exercise for this is to create a circle and lay someone down in the center of the circle. Make sure they are comfortable and warm. Then, from a distance, the group draws the sequence and directs the energy at the person lying in the center. Again, this need only be for 10 minutes. When the healing is over the person nearest the feet simply moves forward and takes the feet in their hands to ground the person. The reaction to this exercise is always amazement as the recipient feels as if they are floating, supported by an energy blanket of love.

The group can then discuss what they felt before the next person lies in the centre.

Beams of energy
Above One of the advantages of Reiki is that it allows you to beam energy across distances.

WORKING ON SPECIFIC ISSUES

Using the distant healing symbols we can target specific issues that prevent us moving forward. For example, we may have issues relating to jealousy or possessiveness that continue to surface in our lives. Even though we are aware of them they prevent us from experiencing happiness and joy in our relationships. We can use Reiki to bring about shifts in our perspective and the way our conditioned responses to a situation cause us to act. It is better to deal with issues one at a time so that you do not over-extend yourself.

Releasing yourself from specific issues
Below You can write out the issue that is affecting you on a piece of paper, empower it with symbols, then release it by burning it.

You will need a lighted candle and a fireproof dish for this exercise. Once you have decided which issue you wish to work on write it down on a piece of paper and sit with it. Examine what the issue means to you. For example, what is jealousy to you? How does it make you feel? What does it look like in someone else? What other times in your life did you feel jealous? Now think of an affirmation that will empower the release of this issue, such as "I am releasing the patterns that create jealousy in my experience". State out loud the affirmation three times. Draw the sequence of symbols to empower your affirmation then light the piece of paper with the candle, place it in the dish, and allow it to burn. Repeat this each day for seven days.

USING THE TELEPHONE

Due to time constraints I am not always able to do one-on-one healing. I find that I spend a lot of time talking through problems with people on the telephone. This modern-day tool is a very simple way to connect to somebody and get a sense of what they are experiencing emotionally. With practice you can empathize as easily over the phone, as if the person was standing right in front of you. I will, therefore, use the phone to connect and simply use the symbol to send healing wherever it is needed. I will often guide the person through the healing on the other end of the phone at the same time. It is a very straightforward and powerful way to work.

Reiki on the telephone
Right You can also practice Reiki over the telephone, sending healing remotely. The recipient can experience this as a rush of heat similar to that experienced in one-on-one Reiki.

Sealing the space
Above A safe environment for the client is created if you "seal" the space before starting the Reiki session.

The power of intention

WHEN THE FIRST LEVEL STUDENTS are asked to comment on their experiences, they talk about how different the experience of giving Reiki can be depending on the situation. If they go through the set procedure to prepare the space, the healing seems more powerful than if the students just lay their hands on somebody without any preparation. Here they are discovering the power of intention. It is the intention we bring to everything we do that is communicated on an energy level. Whether it is cleaning the bath or giving somebody a massage, it is the intent and focus we bring to the task that will affect the final result.

Placing a clear intention into the space I work in is one of the most important aspects of working with energy for me. Once I have done the preparation I feel supported and guided. It is as if a warm jacket of supporting love descends all around me and I am transported to another level of being where my perception, awareness, and sensitivity is taken to a heightened state. I feel I am operating from a place of wisdom. I know I am completely safe and so is anyone entering the space.

After completing the preparation sequence outlined on the facing page, you may feel presences either side of you, and heat or vibration on the side of your face and down your arms. These are the guides who will assist you in your work.

Use the remaining time available to sit quietly with your hands over your heart and solar plexus so that you are open and aware of how you feel. When the client arrives they are usually very aware of the difference in the energy of the room. Sometimes simply entering the room is enough to facilitate an emotional release.

Negative intention

I have experienced the power of intention during a massage. I was lying on the table, without clothes on, feeling vulnerable and putting my well-being in somebody else's hands. The practitioner was distracted and not entirely present. I left the massage with an overwhelming sense of not being appreciated or cared for.

As a rule, good practitioners are very professional and usually that professionalism will include awareness of the importance of being clear and focused in intention.

PREPARATION

- *Arrive 30 minutes before the healing is to take place*
- *Spend a few moments feeling the room to get a sense of what has taken place earlier*
- *Light a candle with the intention of dispelling darkness*
- *Burn frankincense and carry it around the room with the intention of clearing the space of all blocked energy. As you do this you may feel a flood of heat coming into your hands and around your shoulders*
- *Place the power symbol into one corner of the room. Draw the energy along to the next corner and, again, place the power symbol into the corner. Repeat until all four corners are sealed*
- *Seal the entrance to the room with the power symbol*
- *Sit quietly and make your invocation. Call on the Reiki to descend all around you, cleansing and purifying everything within the room. By this time the room will be completely charged with Reiki*

Developing your empathic abilities

Empathic predictions

An interesting aspect of being empathic is that the healer will often feel something before the recipient. They may say: "Are you feeling a pain in your right kidney?" "No" replies the recipient. A few minutes later the recipient will begin to feel pain in the right kidney! These days when the recipient says "No, I don't feel anything in the right kidney" I usually reply, "You will in a while!"

The sceptics among you will say that this is auto-suggestion. However, years of experience have shown me that bringing awareness to an area can reveal hidden issues.

MUCH IS MADE OF THE GIFT OF SEEING ENERGY FIELDS or being clairvoyant, but another gift is more available to everyone and is one of the most accurate tools we have when working with energy. This is our ability to empathize or to be empathic.

The process of initiation in Reiki increases our personal awareness and, therefore, our capacity to empathize. With guidance, a student can become aware of his or her capacity to empathize and develop it as an accurate tool in a relatively short period of time.

To be truly effective, a healer will always have to experience a certain amount of the recipient's pain. This may be felt in many ways, ranging from a wave of emotion to small sensations in the hands as they are passed from position to position. It is not to be confused with taking on someone else's pain. All these sensations are often an accurate reflection of what is going on in the recipient's energy field or physical body. In time, if we allow ourselves to explore these experiences, they will serve to alert us to what is happening in the recipient.

Empathy is a tool that can be honed and perfected to assist you in your work. It will help you discern what is going on energetically in someone you are treating. It is quite common for people to respond to the question of how they are with automatic responses such as, "fine, thanks." At the same time, they may be tied up in knots inside of themselves. It is therefore important to develop your sensitivity so you can see through the illusions that people present to you. This will prove to be useful, not only in treating others, but in discerning your own environment and the people in it. Empathy will become one of your greatest tools, as you begin to listen with your whole body.

Communication without words
Left If we learn to empathize we can communicate on a deeper level, like the special bond that exists between dolphins.

EXERCISES

Take a crystal and sit quietly holding it in your hands. All crystals operate at different frequencies and these can be felt as vibrations. Allow yourself to merge with the crystal until it begins to "talk to you." The vibration usually begins in the hands but will travel through the whole body. With practice, you may find that you can feel where the crystal specifically affects you. If you feel it affects your heart then you have found a crystal for your heart chakra. You may feel emotion or pain in the crystal, particularly if it is unclean or belonged to someone that was in pain. Allow yourself to trust what you are feeling. Once you have mastered feeling crystals you can do the same with objects. Simply hold them and see what happens.

Find a friend and ask them to stand about 10–15 ft (3–4m) in front of you. Allow yourself to relax and simply observe them. Look at how they stand and what defense mechanisms are in place. Focus your attention on them and allow the feelings to come. You may find you don't feel anything. Ask yourself: are they blocking me from getting in? Does their body language reflect this? You may find that you get a sudden pain in your body. Have the confidence to ask if they feel pain in the same place.

The following exercise can be done in your Reiki group. Blindfold one member of the group and then choose a person to give them a hug. Then ask everyone in the room to move around in order to confuse the person in the blindfold. Choose one person to gently guide the blindfolded person around the room, introducing them to everyone. See if he can find the one who hugged him. When you have mastered this try the same exercise without physical contact.

YOU ALWAYS COME FIRST

The practice of giving Reiki involves compassion for others and a willingness to share in their pain. Compassion for oneself and putting your own needs first is a necessary precursor for the effective care of others. It is often the case that those who make themselves available for others forget this simple truth. The nature of giving requires that we balance it with our ability to receive. This simple truth is echoed in Christ's words: "Physician, heal thyself!" It is our own journey that is important, moving beyond the limits that we have in our lives, to always surrender, to dare to be vulnerable and honest about where we are and what we feel. Those we help along the way will benefit all the more from the compassion that we have for ourselves.

Crystals
Above You can use crystals to locate a blockage or problem in a chakra by passing it over your body until you feel an effect. Crystals give out vibrations that help in diagnosis.

Blindfold
Above A blindfold can be used in a valuable exercise to establish empathy and heightened perceptions within your Reiki group.

Energy blockages

REIKI IS NORMALLY CARRIED OUT BY THE LAYING ON OF HANDS to specific areas of the body. In addition, the practitioner may work away from the body in the recipient's energy field. As the practitioner increases in sensitivity, he or she may find that they are able to detect the subtle shifts of energy as they pass their hands through the energy field of the recipient. Through practice and development of our sensitivity we can begin to feel when the shifts we detect are, in fact, energy blockages held in the field. In most cases the hands can simply be held in position where the block is detected and the Reiki will slowly clear the area. Sometimes, however, a little help is required. There are several techniques we can try.

Unblocking tension
Above Energy can be pulled out gently from the client's energy field and thrown into the earth to neutralize it.

Clearing spinal blockages
Above Creating a connection between two points using the fingers will cause energy to flow between the points.

PULLING BLOCKED ENERGY OUT OF THE FIELD

We can use a simple pulling technique to encourage the energy to break up and be pulled from the field of the recipient. When you feel a block in the energy field allow your hand to gently move up and down over the area, feeling for the tension point. This is a little like making energy balls in the palms of your hands. When you feel the tension slowly pull your hand out of the field, making sure the tension is maintained. Once you are away from the field, throw or flick the energy directly into the earth. Never throw it horizontally across a room, or in the direction of someone else, or the energy will contaminate their field. Go back to the same spot and repeat as many times as necessary until you feel the area is clear.

SPINE CLEARING

One of the most common blockages is along the spinal column. This carries the main vertical power current designed to ground energy from spirit. Blockages can occur anywhere along the length of this vertical column, depending on which chakra is being affected at any given time. However the common point that seems to build up pressure is C7 at the base of the neck. This is a common cause of pressure buildup in the head which leads to headache and migraine. The blockage may occur lower down but the pressure backs itself up to this point. To clear, place one finger at the point of C7 and another at the base of the spine. Simply relax and let energy trickle between the two points. The recipient will normally feel this trickle of energy as it travels through the spine and they will sometimes spasm as the block is rapidly released through the energy channels. This feels a little like an electrical shock.

LASER TECHNIQUES

In addition to sending energy from the hand chakras it is possible to use our forefinger and index finger to channel energy. This is especially useful if you wish to be specific in highlighting an area that is blocked. Lightly place your fingers on the area and relax. The Reiki will route itself through them into the recipient's body. Recipients report feeling as if my finger is actually going right through them and moving things around inside their body. This is a useful technique to open up the heart and solar plexus when blocked.

Focusing in
Above Use your fingers as "lasers" to specifically focus on an area.

ENERGY BREAK UP

Sometimes energy blocks need a little encouragement to begin breaking up. In much the same way as a massage therapist will knead the stiff muscle in order to encourage it to relax, so we may employ a similar technique to encourage energy to break up. This technique is done by spreading the fingers of the hands and shaking them from side to side over the blocked area in a rapid movement. This technique is especially useful in the solar plexus and hara area, where energy can become very knotted and stuck. Once the energy begins to move, return to the original method of laying your hand on the area.

Energy breaking
Above Shake the hands in a kneading motion to break up solid blocks of energy, especially in the solar plexus.

BREATH

Breath is your greatest ally when it comes to breaking up old stuck emotional issues. Often a person will be reluctant to breathe into areas that are stuck or stagnated and the breath will appear shallow and weak. Ask the person to open their mouth and breathe in deep fast breaths, in and out of the mouth. Place your hand on the area you wish them to breathe to and support them by matching your breath with theirs. As the area affected is oxygenated old emotions within the cells begin to shift and the person will find that the body takes over the breath control—it becomes automatic. The person will often experience a release of emotions and tingling sensations in their hands as the block begins to move. This technique is quite dramatic and reassurance must be given to the recipient so they feel secure and safe throughout. Once the emotion has been expressed the person will feel very light and free. Allow them to relax for some time and keep them warm with extra blankets. Go to the feet and use the Reiki to ground them.

Breathing
Above Encourage the patient to breathe correctly to stimulate blocked and stagnant areas.

> *"In the life of the spirit, you are always at the beginning."*
>
> RALPH BLUM

Third degree Reiki

THE THIRD DEGREE REIKI COURSE, or master level, is designed for those people who wish to fully embrace the principles of Reiki into their lives, and teach others these principles.

The title "master" simply means that a person has received the final initiation in the Usui system of natural healing and has completed all aspects of that system to a level of understanding which means they can pass it on to others. The master will, hopefully, have learnt enough on his own inner journey to recognize and help others overcome possible pitfalls along their path. The term "master" can be misleading, implying that a person has mastered all aspects of their life. This is not necessarily the case, and discernment is required when choosing a Reiki master to pass on the knowledge to you.

There are certain criteria that a student will have to fulfil in order to participate in the master training. These criteria differ depending on which master you choose, but essentially follow similar guidelines. A master looks for people who have the attributes to make a sympathetic teacher and have embraced the principles of the teachings into their own life. They should have a good understanding of Reiki, practice regularly, and possess the courage and eagerness to continue growing.

At this level, the student teacher relationship becomes very close. Often the student will work alongside the master on a one-to-one basis for a year or more, providing the perfect opportunity to learn the skills necessary to work with groups and pass on the teachings. A financial exchange will take place that reflects the time the master devotes to the student.

The master initiation is usually received over a weekend. Again, how the course is structured depends on the master you choose—some take students to sacred sites or places of significance to make the initiation more memorable. The structure of the weekend should involve receiving the master symbols, the single initiation, and instruction on how to pass on the attunements. A commitment is agreed between the master and student on the work that is to follow. This will include assisting the master in his or her courses, passing on attunements, and helping to organize sharing groups or doing administrative work.

Free as a bird
Above Once you have been initiated as a Reiki master and have run a first and second degree Reiki course under supervision, you are free to teach and heal alone.

When the student master is ready they will teach a course themselves with supervision. Once the student master has successfully run a first and second degree course they are then free to teach alone and are considered a Reiki master. In order to maintain the high standards of Reiki masters, it is important that this apprenticeship is honored.

The master level, like all the stages of Reiki, is a beginning rather than an end. Often a person's choice to become a Reiki master will coincide with big shifts in the way that person chooses to live their life. The choice to become a Reiki master is a choice to assist others in realizing their full potential as human beings.

THE FINANCIAL EXCHANGE

The traditional Usui system considers the financial exchange to be part of the master initiation. This figure was arrived at by Hawayo Takata, the last grand master. At the time it equated to $10,000, which in Japan is seen as a sacred number, though the amount has obviously grown with inflation. It was felt to reflect the student master's understanding of living in an abundant universe where they were able to create what they needed. In other words, if you really believe that you create your own reality go and create $10,000.

This has attracted a lot of criticism from the non-Reiki community, who argue that if Reiki is given to the universe why should we pay for it? But who gave us the trees, the water, the minerals, the flowers, the land, our bodies, or the earth itself? Charging for these things is considered justifiable because they are more tangible.

The issue here is not about paying for Reiki, but rather how we view money, which is merely a form of energy. It has no value of its own, it is simply a form of exchange designed to equate to the energy either given or received. Receiving the master initiation and teachings is a gift of universal proportions and the cost, in comparison, seems quite insignificant.

Money as energy
Below In the traditional Usui system, money is seen as energy. One unit of money, in any currency, equates to one unit of Ki.

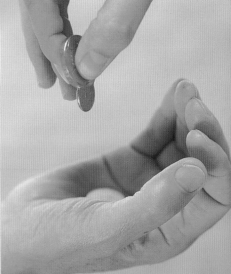

Holding a space for healing

WHEN WORKING ON ANOTHER PERSON it is important to remember that they are facilitating the healing, not the healer. It is very easy to fall into the trap of believing that, as healers, it is our power and expertise that creates the shifts and transformations in others. Nothing could be further from the truth.

It is true that some healers have high awareness, making them more alert to the needs of the person they are treating. This helps them to act at the right time, encouraging the recipient to let go of whatever issues they are holding. But the healer themself cannot physically release these issues. Nor can we force people to go through doors that they are not yet ready for.

When we are alert to another person's situation we are in empathy with them, we are listening. If the recipient is aware of this they will feel supported and be more prepared to work on painful issues. Our responsibilities as healers are simply to listen, open our hearts, and hold the quality of stillness as we channel Reiki. In doing this we hold a space within which another person can transform. The Reiki will be the force that the person uses to create the necessary shift in vibration within their physical, emotional, and mental bodies and, if ready, they will then be able to release whatever they are holding. It is vital that they take responsibility for their own healing to avoid dependency on the healer.

Healing together
Right Through the recognition of another's pain and suffering, we develop compassion. As we watch them heal, a part of us heals with them.

Chapter 5

The seven chakras

Chapter 5

Understanding the seven chakras

If areas of the body's energy field are blocked, a physical disorder can be caused. The Reiki practitioner can use the chakra system as a key to discovering and healing these blockages.

> *"Negative and detrimental thoughts can grow as fast as weeds in a garden and choke all beautiful and delicate flowers if they are allowed to take control"*
>
> EILEEN CADDY

Understanding the seven chakras

REIKI VEIWS DISEASE from an energetic standpoint. Orthodox medical practitioners may see the body as a malfunctioning machine with parts that need to be replaced, cut out, or controlled through medication. The Reiki healer, on the other hand, looks for areas in the energy field that are blocked and restricting the flow of energy to the physical body, thereby causing the physical disorder. These blocks are a form of pollution in the energy field, often the result of unresolved negative emotions or thoughts.

We concentrate on the chakra system in order to understand why a disorder exists and create a positive energetic shift. As we have learned, these energy centers relate to the emotional and psychological make up of a person, as well as to the physical body. The chakras are like a map of a person, holding the history of all that has happened to them.

It is often the case that several chakras are holding pollution and operating dysfunctionally at any one time. A negative loop of experience is then set up, as each dysfunctional chakra affects the others.

THE NEGATIVE LOOP

Trust is a basic psychological theme from the first chakra, the negative aspect being mistrust. If we mate this with a theme from any one of the six other chakras we can see how they coexist to form a dysfunction leading to a negative experience of the secondary chakra characteristic.

For example:

- *Lack of trust + Sexuality* could lead to a negative experience of sexual intimacy
- *Lack of trust + Identity* could lead to an imbalanced view of the self
- *Lack of trust + Love* could lead to an inability to give and receive openly
- *Lack of trust + Communication* could lead to a restriction in the ability to express
- *Lack of trust + Intuition* could lead to a lack of faith in one's own perception
- *Lack of trust + Union* could lead to a pessimistic view of one's place in the universe

As a rule, the first three chakras are the main source of negative pollution in the energy field. This is because the first 20 years of our lives are formative times, when we are at the mercy of outside influences. Any buildup of negative pollution in these three chakras will, in turn, have a negative effect on the chakras that we have yet to develop.

The following pages contain a series of affirmations combined with natural mandalas, which can be used to affirm your relationship with your chakra.

1st Chakra

I am safe, I trust in the natural flow of life.
I take my natural place in the world content in the
knowledge that all I need will come to me in the
right time and space.
I am secure and grounded in the physical form and
give thanks to Mother Earth for the nourishment,
shelter, and stability she gives me.

2nd Chakra

I am a sensuous being.

I express my sexuality fully and freely in all I do.

I celebrate the creative exchange of sexual energy in the universe.

I honor the union and integration of the masculine

and feminine principles as I recognize and

integrate these principles within myself.

I give and receive freely from the wellspring of life.

3rd Chakra

I am at peace with myself and my surroundings.

I express my identity without imposing my will upon others.

I see the differences in others as unique expressions that

contribute more color and fragrance to the world.

I am energized by the light and heat of the sun.

I am in harmony with all I see.

4th Chakra

I am motivated by selflessness.
*   I cultivate the quality of compassion for myself*
*   and all sentient beings.*
I have the willingness to transform pain and suffering
*   in others with the knowledge that, as I do,*
*   I transform pain and suffering within me.*
I have the courage to love unconditionally.

5th Chakra

I am free to express my
creativity with unrestricted enthusiasm and joy.
I give voice to my feelings and communicate
with clarity and openness.
I am a unique being, my opinions are of great value, and
I share them fearlessly.
I am imaginative and colorful in all I do.

6th Chakra

I create my own reality. All experiences that I come into
*   contact with are a reflection of my own*
projected thoughts and emotions.
I develop my inner senses.
*   I am open to new ideas and spiritual concepts.*
My intellectual mind recognizes my intuitive perception.

7th Chakra

I contemplate the impermanent nature of reality.
    I release attachment, recognizing that it is the
        source of all suffering.
I develop emptiness so that I may experience union with the
universal consciousness and merge with the oneness of all creation.
                  I am content.

Chapter **6**

Living with Reiki

"*To see a world in a grain of sand
And a heaven in a wild flower
Hold infinity in the palm of your hand
And eternity in an hour*"

WILLIAM BLAKE

Chapter 6

Living with Reiki

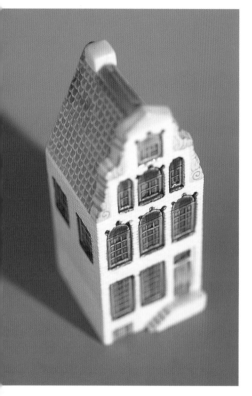

To LIVE WITH REIKI is living with awareness. Whether it is in our home, with our friends, the food we eat, or the work we do: if we carry the awareness of Reiki with us it will bring an element of love to our day-to-day lives. Hawayo Takata once said: "Reiki is unconditional love: when given from one person to another sometimes miracles occur." This is also true of everything we come into contact with. If we treat all those that we meet with respect they will, in turn, respect us. And as we develop compassion for ourselves we find we have more compassion for others.

Applying the Reiki principles on page 122 enhances our ability to flow with the ups and downs of life. If we can pull back from our attachment to a set course of action or outcome and simply allow things to evolve then we are less likely to become stressed. Everything that happens can then be seen as part of our life adventure.

Home
Left Your home reflects who you are. It is a canvas on which you can allow your creativity to express itself.

REIKI IN THE HOME

Everyone has walked into a house and felt its atmosphere. This feeling is made up of the issues and experiences of all who live in or visit that house. If someone holds a strong emotional issue in their field, the home they live in will also contain the essence of their issue.

So our homes are an expression of who we are. If we wish them to reflect the serenity we have found on an inner level, we can use Reiki to do this. Every task we choose to do will carry energy if it is done with awareness of the Reiki energy. Simple tasks, such as doing the dishes, take on a new perspective when we choose to do them with love.

In addition, you can clean each room in your house by invoking the energy and intending it to transform all low vibratory energy within the room. Use the second degree symbols, if you know them, to seal the corners as described on page 81, and apply the same techniques to your home as you would to your healing room.

"Home is where the heart is"

> *"I would be a sad man if it were not for the hope I see in my grandchild's eyes"*
>
> CHIEF DAN GEORGE

REIKI WITH CHILDREN

The child is our teacher and it is best that we remember this fact. For them the veil of forgetfulness is not yet formed—they can still remember where they have just come from. It is a delicate balance to teach a child the ways of the world and yet help them retain the freedom and innocence of youth for as long as possible.

When asked if Reiki is suitable for children I often reply that children *are* Reiki. They are the most vital bundles of energetic love and joy you can find on this planet. If ever I begin to feel the world is a dark place and my heart is heavy, I make a point of watching children to remind myself of the simple joys of living. Only a child can scream in pure ecstasy at simply being alive.

To treat a child with Reiki can prove difficult, simply because children cannot sit still and become bored very easily. Better to wait for them to come to you. Unfortunately, this means they will probably be crying about their grazed knees or cut finger. But most children are resilient by nature and often just need a little rub or kiss from Mom before they are off again shouting and screaming. In these cases Reiki is an excellent option as it works by simply placing your hand on the area that hurts.

Reiki also comes into its own at bedtime, as children will be more receptive to you connecting with them. You may tell stories, or sing to them as you give Reiki.

In the case of more serious illnesses Reiki can, of course, be used alongside any other medication or therapies being administered. In these instances, you may find the time needed to treat children is greatly reduced.

Childhood innocence
Left Children remind us of spontaneity, freedom, and joy. Within our hearts we are all children.

REIKI WITH ANIMALS

Animals, like humans, thrive on touch and they respond to Reiki in the same way that a human being does. There are many people experimenting with Reiki in livestock farming—I have heard of farms in Australia that use Reiki on cattle and seen people using Reiki to calm horses. I have treated many dogs and cats myself, some that healed at an incredible rate as a result.

Animals seem to have a problem sitting still and may, at first, find Reiki an unusual experience. However, once they have received it a few times they will become far more receptive. You will probably find that they start coming to you for regular treatments.

Animals
Above All animals on this planet are our teachers, showing us our connection to the Great Mystery and the intelligence of living in harmony with our environment.

REIKI AND FOOD

Remember it is not only food that we ingest. Each day we feed off a myriad of junk from television, newspaper headlines, politics, advertising, the air we breathe, the water we drink, the thought forms we hear, and so on. It is, therefore, important to pay particular attention to what you take on board your vessel, in both mind and body.

Reiki can have a positive role to play in this aspect of our lives. Through the awareness we gain we can take more responsibility for what we ingest. Once you have awareness of ki the difference in vibration between a

> # "It's not the food that keeps you going, it's the chi in the food."
>
> ### THE BAREFOOT DOCTOR

microwaved hamburger and a lovingly prepared meal with fresh vegetables—if not already obvious—will become startlingly so. The relative benefits of ingesting either one will also be fairly apparent. The choice then is yours. The same goes for what you choose to watch on television, read in newspapers, and so on.

Reiki can also benefit us in our preparation of food. If you imagine that a constant stream of energy is now flowing through you from the universal supply of ki, then everything you touch turns to gold. As you prepare a meal the food will be infused with life-giving ki.

Food
Left Preparing food is a ritual that reminds us of the gifts Mother Earth offers up to us for our security and nourishment.

REIKI WITH PLANTS

Plants operate in the same field of energy as us, so they also benefit from receiving ki to stimulate and nourish them. Plants seem to respond positively to human touch and attention, and when this touch is imbued with the universal ki, the benefits received are multiplied.

I remember a story I was told about an oak tree that stood beside the path to a meditation sanctuary. It had been planted at the same time as all the other oaks in the garden but this one was appreciated on a daily basis. As all the members of the community walked past it on their way to meditation they would remark, "Oh what a lovely oak tree". As a result it had grown at a much faster rate than the others in the garden and appeared more bushy and healthy. It shows us that as we appreciate things they respond and grow stronger and more beautiful.

Plants and Reiki

We can benefit the plants in our home or garden with Reiki. There are some simple methods of doing this.

Carry the awareness of Reiki as you walk around the plants, pruning and watering them. Take time to let the energy flow and send them love.

Before watering the plants hold the container of water in your hands for a few minutes and simply give it Reiki. Allow the ki to infuse the water so that it will contain more nourishment for the plants.

When planting, give Reiki to the roots of the plant before laying it into the ground.

"The complexity of New York City is to a square mile of lowland tropical rain forest as a mouse's squeak is to all the music that has ever been produced by humanity."

DANIEL JANZEN

REIKI WITH THE ELDERLY

Elderly people are often very lonely and isolated in today's society, the world and its people moving too quickly to listen to them. Many elderly people have lost friends, family, or their own partner. Even if they have people to talk to they will most often be deprived of physical touch. Contact with other humans or animals can be deeply nurturing—if we are deprived of it we can feel unloved and emotionally unsupported. This need is acute in some elderly people, especially if they are unable to look after a pet or do not benefit from regular interaction with others.

There are, however, problems that present themselves in treating the elderly. It is difficult to employ techniques such as massage, for example, because of physical frailty or personal inhibitions. Reiki offers a non-intrusive therapy that can be carried out in most environments. And because it re-energizes areas of the body that may be under-exercised, such as stiff or arthritic joints, it can bring enormous benefits and improved quality of life.

Reiki can be used safely with most other medication (see contraindications on page 112) and therefore presents no problems to any care the elderly person may already be receiving. In addition, a person is never too old to change their beliefs about reality and the use of Reiki may present the challenges that stimulate new levels of consciousness. I encourage elderly people to take the first degree Reiki course, as I have seen it bring them a renewed vigor. Young or old, most of us just want to be useful in some way, and age does not affect the body's ability to channel Reiki.

REIKI WITH THE DYING

Death is such a mystery, we know so little about it. Many teachings tell us that it is merely the letting go of your dream self, your physical body, and other self-containing layers of your mortal personality. The destination is a place you are already in—you never left. Christ talked about the vale of forgetfulness to describe living in mortal flesh. This vale is in place to ensure we buy into the illusion of who we think we are. Once the vale is removed at the time of death we remember who we were all along. So the more we identify with our mortal flesh, the harder that transition may be. It could be that we spend our whole lives believing that God doesn't exist, and is merely the deluded imaginings of dreamers, only to find out that God

> **"A little while, a moment of rest upon the wind and another woman shall bear me."**

KAHLIL GIBRAN

does exist and has existed within us all this time. For this reason, I believe it is important to keep an open mind, if only not to look ridiculous at the time of death.

People who develop their awareness through life, particularly through practices such as meditation, are simply working to remove the veil of forgetfulness while still clothed in mortal flesh. At times they may experience breakthroughs in their meditations where they feel the intimate union with all that is. Similarly, people practicing Reiki experience this union on a regular basis, as they are intimately connected to the universal ki. In addition, many Reiki practitioners report feeling or seeing the presence of angelic beings around them when they are working.

For this reason Reiki can have great benefits for those people who are near to this transition themselves. It provides a supportive energy and a quality of experience that is very similar to what they will experience as they move out of denser realms into more vibratory realms. Reiki can help people let go of their attachment to the physical, as it brings them closer to the higher vibratory realms.

When asked to treat people who are terminally ill, remind them that Reiki will assist the person in whichever way they need it most. It may simply help them to move on from this physical experience to the next stage of their infinite adventure.

It is important not to confuse healing with providing a cure. Sometimes the healing may be a shift of awareness that allows a person to open up to their feelings and make peace in their lives before moving on. In the event that death was sudden and unexpected, the second degree symbols can be used to send healing to the person after they have left the body to assist them in overcoming the shock.

Treating the elderly
Above Reiki can be stimulating for the elderly, and may open up whole new areas of their consciousness.

"It is in our defenselessness that we find our greatest protection"

Protection

THIS IS A SUBJECT THAT IS OFTEN TALKED ABOUT by people who are in the process of self development. As we become more sensitive to the subtle energies in the world we also become more aware of the stronger energies. It is not that we suddenly become vulnerable to the world and the people in it, rather that we become aware of the world, the people in it, and the effects our interactions have on us.

I often find that after the first degree course people open up to universal love, and leave the workshop feeling safe and amazed at their own capacity to feel shifts in energy around others, as well as changes in their own fields. Then on Monday morning they head off into work full of enthusiasm, but instead of experiencing universal love they meet resistance in the fields of everyone at work, and sense all the fear, suffering, and unresolved conflicts that these people carry.

THE STONE AND THE FLOWER

The spiritual teacher and Zen Master Osho once described it as the difference in awareness between a stone and a flower. The stone, though alive, is dense and asleep. It has great resilience to the effects of the elements around it. The flower, on the other hand, is vibrant and awake, radiating colors and perfumes into the world. It seems so much more alive than the stone but is vulnerable to the elements and easily damaged. As we become more aware we make the transition from stone to flower. We

Natural differences
Below Our experience is based on our awareness of different vibratory realms. The higher the vibration, the more awareness.

become more vibrant and colorful. We also become more sensitive to the world around us. We might start to feel other people's pain in our own bodies. We may feel exhausted from a simple trip to the city center.

So as we become more aware of ourselves, and get to know what our personal energy feels like, we are far more conscious of the effects that the world and the people in it have on us. This demonstrates the simple truth that our fields change as we release emotional patterns and belief systems. The signature they carry shifts. When we return to familiar situations that previously presented no problems to us, we suddenly can't cope with the experience. It is too painful because we are able to feel the pain that previously we couldn't.

ERECTING BARRIERS

Many people devise all kinds of elaborate ways to protect themselves. These normally involve placing some kind of barrier between themselves and the world. These devices can never be truly effective because their philosophy is wrong.

Let me explain. You are walking down the street feeling at one with the world. Coming in the other direction is a man feeling incredibly angry with the world, closed off and looking for conflict. You feel his pain and anger. You then erect your wall but it's too late. You have felt the pain and anger—it is already in you. Any attempt you make to block it out only serves to block it in. The wall you erected actually traps his feelings within you. As you placed your protection between yourself and his anger and pain, you actually created separation between his experience and your own. You made a judgement of him and decided that you wanted to exclude him from your experience. The oneness you were experiencing previously didn't include him. But of course it does—we are all one. He is a part of you.

Oneness
Above There is no separation other than the separation created in your mind. Every person you meet is an expression of the same being.

ACCEPTING OTHERS

So what do we do? To answer, I will recount an experience that I believe I was given to teach me this principle.

In 1995 I was living in a spiritual community in the north of Scotland, surrounded by supportive and loving people. I had to visit London for a seminar so found myself on the Underground in the center of town. We

A containment exercise

Before leaving the house in the morning, this simple exercise will help you gather yourself.

Imagine that a powerful magnet sits one inch below your belly button, and this magnet is designed to attract only the energy that belongs to you. Your belly button is the switch. Press the switch, turn on the magnet, and visualize all the parts of yourself returning to you from wherever they may be. Once you are complete, imagine a belt of light activating from your base chakra and spinning anticlockwise around you, passing through each chakra on its way up to your crown. Use the affirmation "I am the presence activating my electronic belt at the speed of light now". This belt will contain all your energy, and will help you to maintain your center and boundaries.

pulled into a station and, as the doors opened, I felt a ripple of fear go through me. I noticed that the same ripple went right down the train, affecting everyone on it. The next moment a huge man entered the train. He was drunk, very angry, and looking for someone to challenge him. He came over to where I was sitting, threw the man who was sitting opposite me off the seat, and sat down.

Everyone on the train was trying to shrink into a corner, such was the power of this man's projections. He started to loudly sing songs that were designed to insult everyone on the train.

After his first song he looked at me. I found myself able to hold his gaze, even though I wanted to look away and hide like everyone else on the train. I noticed that he was enjoying himself. As I looked at him I felt myself accepting him for who he was and empathizing with him. I felt fear but I knew it wasn't mine—it was his fear.

He asked me what I thought of his song. I told him that it was an angry song. He replied: "Of course it was an angry song, I'm an anarchist." He sang another song and looked back at me and, almost as if he realized that I was his friend, he held out his hands—they were covered in scratches and blood—and said he had hurt himself. I took hold of one of his hands and the fear in me dissolved. I was holding the hands of a scared young man who wanted love and attention, not an angry man who might hurt me.

The rest of the journey was uneventful. When his stop arrived he got up, said goodbye, and left. It was only then that I noticed the rest of the people on the train. They were all staring at me as if I had disarmed a man with a machine gun.

When I left the train I felt rushes of ecstasy through my body as the whole experience—all the fear, anger, and sadness—left me. This taught me that if we are prepared to experience others fully, and do not engage in conflict with them, they cannot hurt us and, when we move out of their fields, the experience lifts off us effortlessly.

Being open and developing yourself means that you will feel the pain of those who have not yet made the choice to re-connect to their hearts and feelings. When this pain becomes a burden to you it is important to know that it is a warning. Retreat and take time to re-center and balance yourself.

Closing down after healing

JUST AS WE GO TO GREAT LENGTHS to prepare and open ourselves for healing so we must also close down again afterward and make sure we disengage from the person we are working with. This serves to close our crown, which will be open after healing, and disengage from our client to avoid them becoming dependent on us as healers. This is simply done through a combination of intention and visualization.

As you finish working with your client, place your hands on their shoulders if they are sitting, or the feet if they are lying down. Thank your guides for helping you and slowly detach from the person. Now go and wash your hands. As you wash work through the following visualization:

Imagine each chakra is a flower. Each flower is the color of the corresponding chakra, red for base, orange for sacral, and so on. Starting with the crown, see the flower as brilliant and open, then close it so that it becomes a bud. Continue through each chakra until they are all closed.

Cold water
Washing the hands in cold water after Reiki helps to remove energy taken on from the client, and to disengage from them.

Protect yourself

• The main awareness you need to carry for protection is the knowledge that you are safe. Think of the sun—it continues to shine, unaffected by the darkness around it.

• Being centered, grounded, and open-hearted can also help when dealing with external conflict.

1 Ensure you are grounded. Simply focus your awareness downwards and feel the earth supporting you. Open up your base center. Shift your awareness from your solar plexus, where you will be experiencing the conflict, and focus your awareness on your heart center.

2 Breathe into your heart and imagine the center expanding and opening. You may feel warmth enter it as you do this.

3 Observe the person you want to protect yourself from and remember that any negative behaviour is simply a survival response because, at some time, they have not received love. Send love from your heart and simply think "I accept you as you are, you are a part of me".

Exercising caution

THERE ARE FEW CONTRAINDICATIONS to worry about when giving Reiki. In
most cases, following these simple precautions will ensure a safe treatment.

- *Always ensure that broken bones are set in a cast before giving
  Reiki. This is because Reiki's efficiency to heal bones is remarkable
  in the early stages of a break, and if the bone is not set properly it
  may heal incorrectly.*
- *Caution should be taken when treating people with heart problems,
  especially if they have been fitted with artificial devices such as
  pacemakers, as Reiki may affect the device itself.*
- *Pregnant women should always be treated with care, particularly
  in the early stages of pregnancy. Most alternative therapies advise
  caution in this situation and Reiki is no exception.*
- *Care should be taken when treating people with diabetes. Reiki has
  been shown to affect the levels of insulin required by the body, so
  simply warn the recipient that they need to monitor their insulin
  levels closely if they are to receive treatments.*
- *Always reduce the length of treatments on children. Usually they
  will become restless when they have had enough.*
- *Avoid giving Reiki after drinking alcohol.*
- *Avoid giving Reiki to anyone who is under the influence of alcohol
  or drugs.*

> **"*One love, one heart, let's get together and feel all right*"**
>
>
>
> BOB MARLEY

Reiki and other therapies

PHYSICAL THERAPIES

Jennifer Gresty has been a practitioner for ten years, specializing in deep tissue massage. She is a qualified reflexologist and aromatherapist and has taught ITEC therapeutic massage for five years. This is her experience of Reiki.

"I had been interested in doing a Reiki course for some time although I really didn't expect it to create a big shift for me, even though I wanted to work on a deeper level. I am astounded by the degree in which Reiki has affected my life, not only in my work but also on a personal level. It brought a lot of deep issues to the surface and has enabled me to pass through emotional crossroads. It has helped me to accept who I am and empowered me to change aspects of my life. It has helped me value myself. I feel far more grounded and have the desire to meditate more with more focus in my meditations. I feel more guided in my whole life and, in some way, safer. I have this profound sense of security.

"After the Reiki course I felt like I had been plugged in. My work has been enhanced beyond belief, and I have been able to break through boundaries with certain clients that I would have been unable to do before.

"When I go into a session now I am far more aware of tuning in, and the difference this makes to the energy in the room. I am looking more at the distortions that may exist in the chakras and energy of the person and am in empathy with the person I am working on.

"When I have time I will use Reiki at the beginning of a session to calm the client down, which gives me a real sense of what they need or what is going on for them. If someone has a specific area of pain during a treatment I will often stop massaging and simply pour Reiki into that area to help move the block. Many of my clients have remarked that they feel more relaxed than when they previously received massage.

"Reiki has been a great asset to me. My advice to other physical therapists who wish to work on a deeper level would be to attend a Reiki course up to second degree, as it would greatly enhance their work."

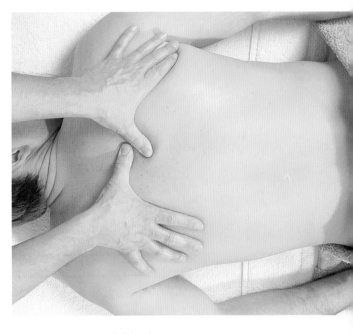

Reiki and massage
Above Combining Reiki with deep tissue massage can give a deep sense of security both to the practitioner and the patient.

Living with Reiki • 113

ACUPUNCTURE

Sue Johnson has been an acupuncturist for ten years and is a clinical tutor at the British College of Acupuncture. In 1996 she attended one of my seminars in London.

"As an acupuncturist I often felt that there was more I could be doing to speed up the healing process, rather than just pop in needles and sit back. I wanted to be more involved and would often sit close to the client and talk to them, trying to unearth information that would allow me to gain a greater understanding of their process. A few years after qualifying I went to a seminar by an eminent Chinese doctor, John Shen, who was 86 years old and wanted to pass on some of his vast experience. One sentence stood out from the whole day: "Acupuncture is 10% technique and 90% spirit."

"From that day I searched to find out how to 'heal'. I went to many seminars, read many books, and tried many techniques. I was at the point of giving up when Richard (the author) phoned me out of the blue to tell me he wanted to teach me something that would enhance my treatments. That something turned out to be Reiki.

"Acupuncture works by re-balancing the energy already in the body. I often found myself trying to manipulate low levels of energy, spending weeks building up these levels by stimulating the digestive system to draw more from food. By flooding the system with Reiki I can produce changes more rapidly. It is a little like a central heating system. If air gets into the system the radiators are left half cold. If we release the air by adding more water, the system works again.

"Another hurdle to overcome in treating people with acupuncture is long-held mental and emotional attitudes. These need to be shifted in order for the body to maintain health. These shifts would normally take years, but with Reiki I find these old patterns that

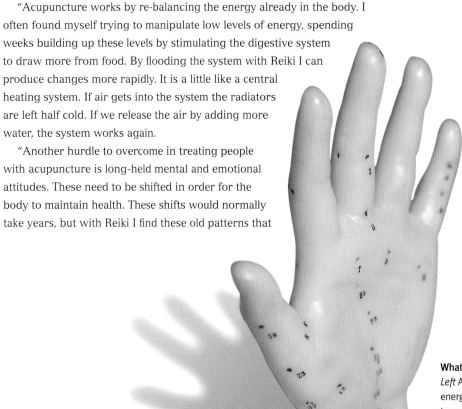

What is acupuncture?
Left Acupuncture utilizes the ki energy within the body and works to redistribute it, creating a deep sense of harmony in the mind, body, and spirit.

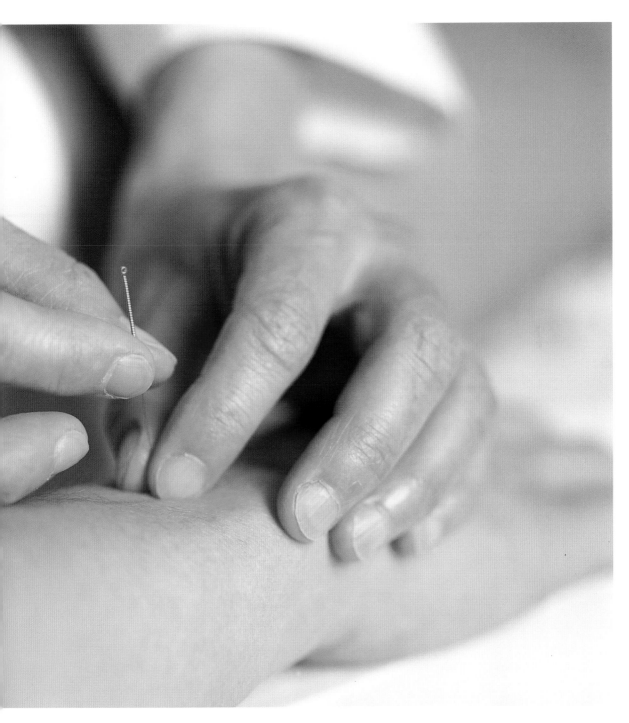

have locked themselves inside the structure of the body can be lifted out.

"In the past month I have seen three young women in their late 20s with similar gynaecological conditions. Interestingly, all three lost their mothers between the ages of 10 and 14, just the time that the second chakra is developing. Reiki has been of enormous benefit in bringing these old memories and emotions to the surface in order for the healing to take place in their physical bodies."

Reiki and acupuncture
Above If used in conjunction with Reiki, acupuncture can be an even more effective method of healing. Here, channels are opened in the meridian system using pins.

Kirlian photography healing test

FOR MANY YEARS healers have talked about their ability to manipulate the energy fields around patients to facilitate healing. Up until now we have been unable to prove this fact and have had to rely on our own faith in what we do. Today, however, the Gas Discharge Visualization machine, invented by Dr. K. Korotkov in Russia, is able to produce a representation of the human energy field utilizing state of the art computer, electronic, and optic technology.

Here, we took photographs of a woman's energy field before and after healing. I gave a short treatment between photographs for approximately 20 minutes and observed the changes that took place in the field.

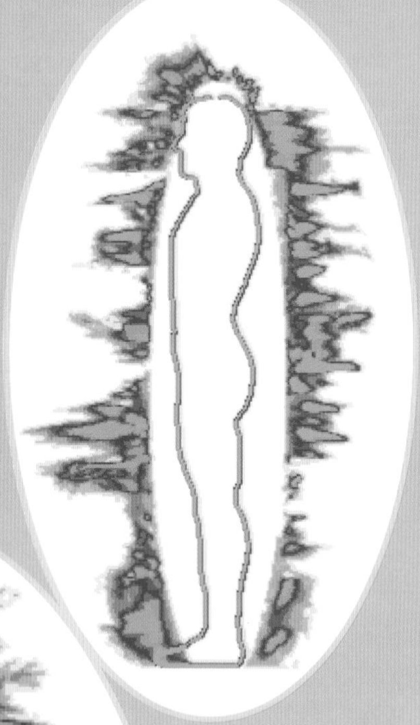

Left side

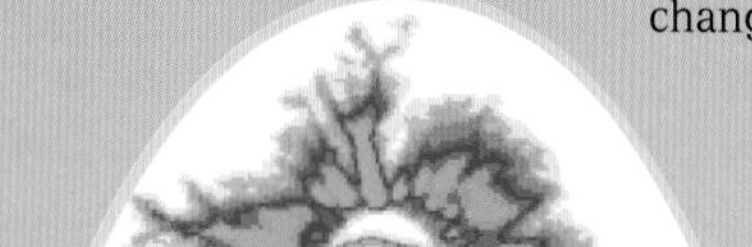

Right side

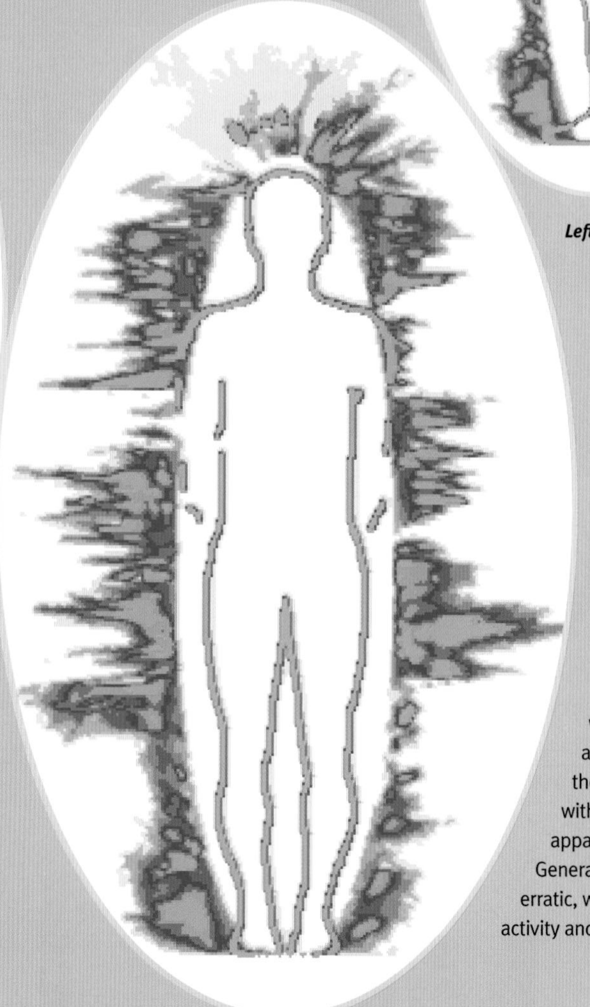

Front

Before healing
This reveals that the front, left, and right sides of the energy field have strong gaps in the second, third, and fifth chakras. The left emotional side is weaker than the right and this is reflected in the right side of her brain, with a strong weakness apparent in the field. Generally, the field looks erratic, with areas of both over-activity and under-activity.

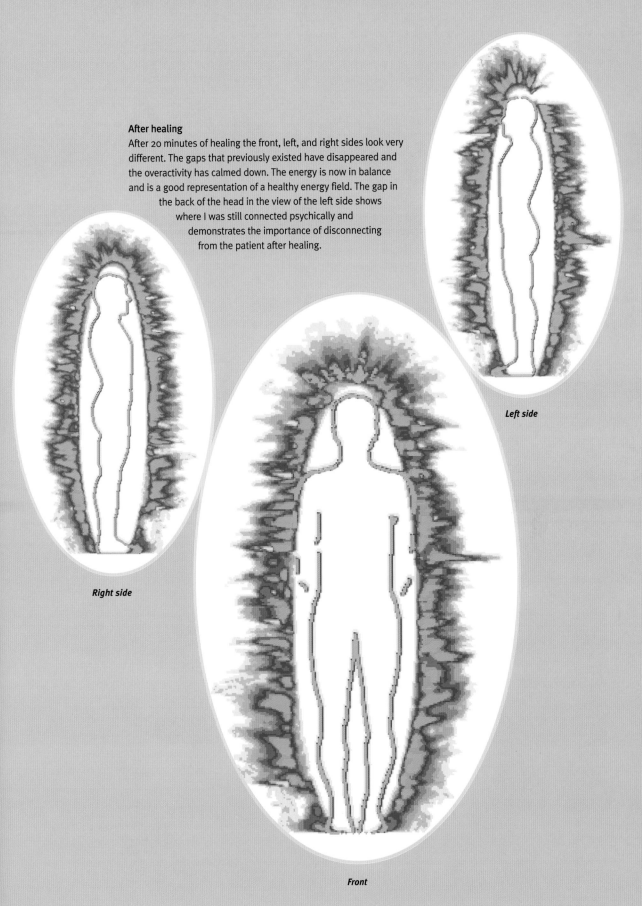

After healing
After 20 minutes of healing the front, left, and right sides look very different. The gaps that previously existed have disappeared and the overactivity has calmed down. The energy is now in balance and is a good representation of a healthy energy field. The gap in the back of the head in the view of the left side shows where I was still connected psychically and demonstrates the importance of disconnecting from the patient after healing.

Left side

Right side

Front

The origins of Reiki

DR. USUI

Dr. Mikao Usui, the founder of the Usui system of natural healing, was born in Japan in the mid-19th Century. He lived in the city of Kyoto and worked as a minister and teacher at a Christian school for boys. It was during one of his classes that he was asked a question that was to change his life. One of the boys questioned if he believed in the stories told in the bible of the healing miracles that Jesus performed. Dr. Usui replied that he did. The boy replied that he would seek proof of the stories, rather than simply believe what is written in the bible.

Dr. Usui, unable to get this question out of his mind, felt challenged to go out into the world to seek proof of Jesus's healing miracles. It is said that he first traveled to the USA and lived in Chicago, where he studied theology and Sanskrit, before returning to Japan seven years later. There he studied ancient sutras and traveled around many Buddhist monasteries. He finally met an abbot who encouraged him to keep up the search and study the original Buddhist sutras in Sanskrit text. He found mention of methods of healing, but no information that could enable him to activate or access healing energy.

The abbot recommended that he go inward for the answers, through prayer and meditation. Dr. Usui set off on a 21-day fast and retreat on the top of the sacred mountain Kuri Yama, near Kyoto. After climbing the mountain Dr. Usui sat facing east and laid out 21 stones before him. Each day he threw a stone away to keep track of the passing days.

In the early hours of the 21st day he prayed in earnest for the answers to his questions. As he did so he saw a light moving towards him from across the valley. He felt that this was the answer, and opened himself up to accept it despite his fear. The light struck him in his third eye (sixth chakra) on the forehead. Dr. Usui was immediately taken into an altered state of color, light, and energy. Symbols, and their meaning, were presented to

Usui's mountain vision
Below Reiki was born through the vision Dr. Usui saw while fasting and meditating on the sacred mountain Kuri Yama near Kyoto in Japan.

him, and he was shown how to activate healing energy in all who wished it. He heard the words "Remember remember".

Dr. Usui awoke from his vision to find it was already light. Much time had passed while he had been experiencing the vision. Despite not eating for 21 days he felt full of energy and excitement and started running down the mountain. But, in his haste, he fell and cut his toe. He held his foot in his hand and was amazed as the bleeding stopped, and his toe was healed after just a few minutes. He continued down the mountain until he came to an inn, where he ordered some food. On hearing that he had been fasting the proprietor cautioned him against eating, but Dr. Usui ignored him and ate to satisfy his hunger, suffering no indigestion. The proprietor's grand daughter had toothache and was in great pain. Dr. Usui placed his hands on her jaw and the pain disappeared. He continued on his journey and, upon arriving at the monastery, found the abbot suffering from arthritic pain. Again, Dr. Usui laid his hands on the abbot and the pain went away.

The first Grand Master
Above Dr. Mikao Usui, founder of the Usui system of natural healing known throughout the world today as Reiki.

Dr. Usui decided that he would begin working with the new-found energy in the Beggars' Quarter in Kyoto. He lived and worked there every day, treating people by laying his hands on them. He soon realized that the people were not taking responsibility for their lives and that, despite the support and encouragement he gave them, they returned to begging on the streets. When he asked them why they simply said that it was easier to beg.

Dr. Usui was deeply discouraged by this and chose to lay down the five principles of Reiki. He concentrated his efforts on teaching healing so that people could take responsibility for their own lives. Dr. Usui is said to have initiated 16 masters in Reiki and he entrusted one of these, Dr. Chujiro Hayashi, to maintain the teachings after his death.

The second Grand Master *Right* Dr Chujiro Hayashi, founder of the first Reiki clinic in Tokyo, Japan, developed the hand positions and the three levels of Reiki.

DR. CHUJIRO HAYASHI

Dr. Hayashi was a retired naval officer with a deep interest in spiritual practices. After becoming a Reiki master at the age of 47 he opened a clinic in Tokyo and devoted his life to training others in Reiki. His clinic thrived, with practitioners working in groups on patients. Dr. Hayashi established the Reiki positions and the three levels of Reiki, devising an initiation for each level. He was a renowned psychic and, sensing the coming conflict of the Second World War, he felt it important to preserve the knowledge he had been given. He passed the mantle of responsibility to a Japanese woman living in Hawaii, by the name of Hawayo Takata, who had entered his life many years earlier as a patient at his Tokyo clinic.

HAWAYO TAKATA

Born on the island of Kauai on December 24 1900, Hawayo Takata's parents were Japanese immigrants, her father working in the sugar cane fields. She married Saichi Takata, the bookkeeper for the plantation, and they had two daughters. Saichi died in 1930, leaving Mrs. Takata to raise their children.

Life was not easy for Hawayo and she had to work hard to provide for her family. She developed nervous exhaustion and severe abdominal pain. Soon after, one of her sisters died and Hawayo traveled to Japan to deliver the news to her parents. While there her condition deteriorated and she went to hospital. It was found that she had a tumor, gallstones, and appendicitis. She needed an operation.

While being prepared for the anaesthetic Hawayo heard a voice, which told her that the operation was not necessary. She knew she was wide awake, and had not imagined the voice, but had not experienced anything like this before. She asked a doctor if he knew of any other way that she could be healed. The doctor told her about Dr. Hayashi's Reiki clinic.

On visiting the clinic Hawayo was impressed by the Reiki practitioner's ability to detect problem areas simply by scanning the body with his hands. The heat from his hands was so strong that she believed he must be using some sort of equipment and tried to grab the sleeves of his kimono to see what he was concealing. The practitioner was startled but once Hawayo explained her misgivings, he began to laugh. He told her about Reiki and how it worked.

The third Grand Master
Below Hawayo Takata, founder of the payment structure of Reiki and responsible for the expansion of Reiki to the West.

Mrs. Takata received daily treatments and her condition improved. In four months, she was completely healed. She was impressed with these results and wanted to learn Reiki. In the spring of 1936, Mrs. Takata received first degree Reiki. She worked with Dr. Hayashi for one year before receiving second degree Reiki.

Mrs. Takata returned to Hawaii in 1937 and was initiated as a Reiki master by Dr. Hayashi soon after. He then announced that he wished her to be his successor.

Hawayo Takata somehow escaped incarceration as a Japanese American during the war. By the time of her death on December 11 1980, she had initiated 22 Reiki masters. She named Phyllis Lei Furumoto, her grand daughter, as her successor.

The five spiritual principles of Reiki

THESE PRINCIPLES were put in place by Dr Usui, the founder of the Usui system of natural healing, shortly after he had been working with beggars on the streets of Kyoto. He had decided that he needed to give guidelines to the people he worked with in order for them to live a more fulfilled life. The guidelines constitute ways in which we can take more responsibility for our lives and, although they were written over 100 years ago, they are still relevant today.

JUST FOR TODAY DO NOT WORRY

This principle reminds us that we must trust in the process of life. When we worry, it is often because we have become caught in the confusion of our outer experience and have become fearful of the future. Our fear leads us to attempt to control all aspects of our lives, rather than trusting in the natural abundance and security that comes from being in our natural place. When we worry we send our fears out into the world, and when the world reflects them the spiral of confusion gains momentum in our lives. Instead, try to relax and know that what is yours will come to you at the right time.

JUST FOR TODAY DO NOT ANGER

When we feel anger it is often because we have given away our power, or failed in some way to express our needs. The outer world is a reflection, so if we find ourselves angry with someone they are often only doing us a service and showing us what needs attention in our own lives. We are, in fact, angry with ourselves for failing to take the action that would have prevented the situation arising in the first place.

HONOR YOUR PARENTS, TEACHERS, AND ELDERS

It is easy to lay the blame for all that is wrong in our lives at the door of our parents, teachers, or elders. If we are able to rise up and see life from a greater perspective then we can realize that everyone in our lives is there for a reason. Those who give us the greatest lessons are those that love us the most. It is important to recognize that nothing happens by chance: you have chosen your parents and your life situation in order to experience the very difficulties you need to grow. Love them and honor them for being part of your experience.

EARN YOUR LIVING HONESTLY

Through our work we express ourselves. When we receive payment for what we do we learn to respect ourselves and take responsibility for our lives. It is important that we find our place in the world and express our unique gifts.

SHOW GRATITUDE TO EVERYTHING

Never take anything for granted. Instead, give thanks for every meal you eat, every day you live, every prayer that is answered. Life is so very precious and, as we learn to appreciate our own life, we will learn to appreciate all life.

Resource Directory

Richard Ellis
e-mail: r161165@ix.netcom.com

British Reiki Association
2 Manor Cottages
Stockley Hill
Peterchurch
Hereford, UK
HR2 OSS
Tel: (UK) 01981 550 829

Kirlian Research Ltd
4th Floor, 25–27 Oxford Street
London, UK
W1R 1RF
Tel: (UK) 0171 287 7980
Fax: (UK) 0171 287 7963
e-mail: ElenaT@bigfoot.com
http://www.kirlian.co.uk

The Reiki Alliance
P.O. Box 41
Cataldo, ID 83810
USA

Reiki Touch Master Foundation
P.O. Box 571785
Houston, TX 77057
USA

Reiki Outreach International
Mary A. McFadden
P.O. Box 609
Fair Oaks, CA 95628
USA
Tel: (US) 916 863 1500
Fax: (US) 916 863 6464

International Association of Reiki Professionals
P.O. Box 481
Winchester, MA 01890
Tel: (US) 781 729 3530
Fax: (US) 781 721 7306
e-mail: info@iarp.org

Canadian Reiki Association
P.O. Box 40026
Marlee, Toronto
Ontario M6B 4K4
Canada
Tel: (Canada) 416 783 9904
Fax: (Canada) 416 242 6819
Website:
http://ourworld.compuserve.com/homepages/can
adian_reiki_assn/homepage.htm

Australasian Independent Reiki Practitioners Association Inc.
P.O. Box 1483
Armidale, NSW 2350
Australia
Tel: (Australia) 2 6775 5544
Fax: (Australia) 2 6775 5579
e-mail: reiki@northnet.com.au

International Association of Reiki-Main office
Lesni 14
46001 Liberec
Czech Republic
Tel/fax: (Czech Republic) 048 424 629
e-mail: reiki@lbc.pvtnet.cz

Index

Credits

Thanks to all at Quarto Publishing plc for their support and guidance in writing this book.

Special thanks to:

Sarah Vickery for editing my material into readable form
Sally Bond for all her hard work in the art department
Ruth Hope for her wonderful design work.

Also thanks to:

Sue Johnson
Jennifer Gresty
Jenny Gardy
for their contributions.
Hina Patel for agreeing to participate in the Kirlian photography experiment.
Elena Tchernychko at Kirlian Research Ltd for the experiments with The Gas Discharge Visualisation Machine.
Sue Parkinson for her wonderful hair and make-up, friendship, and moral support.
The Kailash Centre of Oriental Medicine for letting us use their space to take the photographs.
The photographer **Paula Zucchi**, assistant **Ann Burke** and models **Chrissy Dean** and **Geoff Burton**.
June Woods for being a great source of inspiration and for being such a loving example for me to follow.
Alessandra Beretta for her selfless contributions to all my workshops.
Angeles Costa for being an angel.
Melanie Probert for teaching me to appreciate every flower I see.

Tony Palmeri and **Matthew Sanderson** for being brothers.
Eddie and **Lucy** for being so beautiful, and for their sofa bed.
Jenny Martin and **Michael Harkness** for living with me and surviving.
Perluigi for his jokes and cappuccinos.
Sabrina for her deep friendship.
All my students for trusting me.
Laura for her love.
Finally, my family for all the fun times we've had together.

Thanks also to anyone I have forgotten to mention who has helped me along the way.

Picture Credits

Quarto Publishing plc. would like to thank and acknowledge the following for providing pictures reproduced in this book:

Richard Ellis 35, 36, 93, 94, 95, 96, 97, 98, 99
Image Bank 26, 82, 86, 109
Pictor International 106

The photographs on pages 119, 120, and 121 are reproduced with the permission of Phyllis Lei Furumoto.

All other photographs are the copyright of Quarto Publishing plc.